FOR YOUR EYES ONLY

BEN MACINTYRE is a columnist and Associate Editor on *The Times*. He has worked as the newspaper's correspondent in New York, Paris and Washington. He now lives in London with his wife and three children. *Agent Zigzag*, the true story of a WWII double-agent, was a recent *Sunday Times* bestseller.

FOR YOUR EYES ONLY

Ian Fleming + James Bond

Ben Macintyre

B L O O M S B U R Y

LONDON · NEW DELHI · NEW YORK · SYDNEY

First published in Great Britain 2008
This paperback edition published 2009

Copyright © 2008 by Ben Macintyre

Chapters 9 and 10 originally appeared in *The Times*,
copyright: Times Newspapers Ltd

Bloomsbury Publishing Plc
50 Bedford Square
London WC1B 3DP

www.bloomsbury.com

Bloomsbury Publishing, London, New Delhi, New York, and Sydney

A CIP catalogue record for this book is available from the British Library

ISBN 978 0 7475 9866 4
10 9 8 7 6 5

Illustrations by Grade Design Consultants, London
www.gradedesign.com

Typeset by Hewer Text UK Ltd, Edinburgh
Printed in Great Britain by CPI Group (UK) Ltd CR0 4YY

MIX
Paper from
responsible sources
FSC
www.fsc.org   FSC® C020471

FOR YOUR EYES ONLY

Ian Fleming + James Bond

CONTENTS

CONTENTS

AUTHOR'S NOTE

This book, published to coincide with a major exhibition at the Imperial War Museum in London, is a homage to Ian Fleming on the centenary of the author's birth, and a celebration of James Bond, his greatest creation. It is not a biography of Ian Fleming – others, notably John Pearson and Andrew Lycett, have already performed that task admirably – nor is it a 'biography' of James Bond, for that, too, has been written. It does not purport to be a comprehensive guide to the James Bond phenomenon (for this, I recommend Henry Chancellor's official companion). Rather, it is a personal investigation into the intersection of two lives, one real and one fictional.

As a journalist and writer of non-fiction, I have always been intrigued by the factual origins of fiction. In previous books, I went in search of the nineteenth-century criminal Adam Worth, the model for Professor Moriarty in the Sherlock Holmes tales, and Josiah Harlan, an adventurer who would win literary immortality in Rudyard Kipling's short story 'The Man Who Would Be King'. All novelists find inspiration in reality, but Ian Fleming, more than any writer I know, anchored the imagined world of James Bond to the people, things and places he knew. Espionage is itself a shadowy trade between truth and untruth, a complex interweaving of imagination, deception and reality. As a former officer in naval intelligence, Fleming thought like a spy, and wrote like one. This book is an attempt to explore a remarkable double life and to establish, as nearly as possible, where the real world of Ian Fleming ended and the fictional world of James Bond begins.

Ben Macintyre, April 2008

001

'THE SCENT AND SMOKE AND SWEAT OF A CASINO . . .'

'The scent and smoke and sweat of a casino . . .'

One morning in February 1952, in a holiday hideaway on the island of Jamaica, a middle-aged British journalist sat down at his desk and set about creating a fictional secret agent, a character that would go on to become one of the most successful, enduring and lucrative creations in literature. The circumstances were not immediately auspicious. Ian Fleming had never written a novel before, though he had done much else. He had tried his hand at banking, stock-broking and working as a newspaper correspondent. As a young man of English privilege, he had toyed with the idea of being a soldier, or a diplomat, but neither had worked out. Only during the war, working in the Intelligence Division of the Royal Navy, had he found a task – as an officer in naval intelligence dreaming up schemes to bamboozle the enemy – worthy of his vivid imagination. But by 1952, the excitement of the war was just a memory. He had settled into a job as a writer and manager on the *Sunday Times*, a role that involved some enjoyable travel, a little work and a lot of golf, women and lunch. Born to wealth and status, Ian Fleming found his existence undemanding but unsatisfying. Even his best friends would have snorted at the notion that he was destined for immortality.

This, then, was the man who, after a morning swim to wash out the hangover of the night before, hunched over the desk in his Jamaican home 'Goldeneye' and began to type, using six fingers, on his elderly Royal portable typewriter. The opening line, after several amendments and corrections, would read: 'The scent and smoke and sweat of a casino are nauseating at three in the morning . . .' Fleming wrote fast, the words pouring out at the rate of two thousand a day, crammed into the space between dawn and the first cocktail, a great rush of creativity conceived in haste and a miasma of tobacco smoke.

A month after he had started writing, Fleming tapped out the words '. . . "the bitch is dead now".' *Casino Royale* was complete, and James Bond was born.

Like the character he had created, Ian Fleming was a great deal more complex than he seemed on first acquaintance. Beneath the sybaritic exterior, Fleming was a driven man, intensely observant, with an internal sense of romance and drama that belied his public languor and occasional cynicism. He pretended not to take his books too seriously – 'the pillow fantasies of an adolescent mind' was how he later described them – but he approached the craft of thriller-writing with the precision of a professional, and he knew, instinctively, exactly what he was doing. He wrote for many reasons: to take his mind off his impending marriage to Ann Rothermere; increasingly, to prove to her somewhat snooty literary friends that he was a genuine novelist; to emulate his brother, the successful travel writer Peter Fleming; and to stop his friend and neighbour in Jamaica, Noël Coward, from badgering him to get on and 'write his bloody book'. He also wrote to make money, preferably in large quantities. Fleming liked money (his lifestyle demanded it), and never felt he had quite enough. James Bond would soon help to put that right.

However, for all Fleming's apparent insouciance, this was no mere money-making venture, but an expression and extension of an extraordinary man. Bond is, in part, Fleming. The exploits of 007 grew directly out of Fleming's knowledge of wartime intelligence and espionage; they shared similar tastes and attitudes towards women; they even looked similar. Fleming would teasingly refer to the Bond books as 'auto-biography'. Like every good journalist, Fleming was a magpie, collecting material avidly and continuously: names, places, plots, gadgets, faces, restaurant menus and phrases; details from reality that would then be translated into fiction. He once remarked: 'Everything I write has a precedent in truth.' Fleming's research extended to his own personality, which would find expression in a handsome, attractive and conflicted secret agent.

But Bond is also, in part, what Fleming was not. He was the fantasy of what Fleming would like to have been – indeed, what every Englishman raised on Bulldog Drummond and wartime derring-do would like to have been. Bond is a grown-up romantic fairy tale, a promise that Britain, having triumphed in the World War, was still a force to be reckoned with in the dull chill of the Cold War. In the grim austerity of postwar Britain, here was a man dining on champagne and caviar, enjoying guiltless sex, glamorous foreign travel, and an apparently unlimited expense account.

This was the Bond recipe: part imagination and part truth; part Ian Fleming and part his alter ego; fiction based on fact, with a dash of journalism. This thriller cocktail was as heady and intoxicating as the weapons-grade martini James Bond orders in *Casino Royale*: 'Three measures of Gordon's, one of vodka, half a measure of Kina Lillet. Shake it very well until it's ice cold, then add a large thick slice of lemon-peel.' Kina Lillet was a particularly bitter wine-based aperitif laced with quinine from the bark of the South American cinchona tree, or 'kina kina'; vodka mixed with gin is a particularly lethal combination. Drinking one of these Bond cocktails is a little like reading one's first Bond novel: it leaves you reeling, light-headed and faintly guilty, but keen for another.

Casino Royale contains many of the ingredients that explain why Bond would go on to conquer the world: beautiful, externally tough but emotionally vulnerable women; a glamorous setting; a repulsive villain; cold-blooded communist killers; sex, violence and luxury. But it is the character of Bond – established in the first novel and hardly altered thereafter – that explains the enduring appeal of the world Fleming forged: tough, resourceful, quintessentially British, but also, as Fleming intended, empty – the blunt instrument of the British secret service, a blank slate for the reader to write on.

Thirteen more Bond books would follow *Casino Royale*. By the time of his death, just twelve years later, Ian Fleming had sold more than forty million copies, and the first two Bond films had been made, to acclaim, giving birth to a multi-billion-dollar industry that expands with every passing year. Today, more than half the world's population has seen at least one Bond film. Ann, Fleming's wife, would nickname him 'Thunderbeatle', as rich and celebrated as the Beatles themselves. Bond not only outlived Fleming, but continues to be reborn: new films, new books authorised by the Fleming estate, new spoofs. Every age gets the Bond it needs. He is updated with new attitudes to sex, smoking and alcohol, and remodelled with fresh tailoring, new enemies and ever more imaginative gadgets. The film Bond evolved in different ways from Fleming's creation, taking on the characteristics of actors as different as Sean Connery, George Lazenby, Roger Moore, Timothy Dalton, Pierce Brosnan and now

Daniel Craig. In the books, Bond kills sparingly, while on screen the carnage is often staggering. Fleming's Bond is vulnerable, prey to nerves and even fear, whereas on screen he barely bleeds, let alone psychologically. Yet the essential Bond is the same, the brand eternal: a sardonic, stylish, seductive Englishman, with a licence not just to kill, but to perform every feat that an armchair Bond can imagine.

Back in 1952, having finished what he called his 'oafish opus', Fleming stuck the sixty-thousand-word manuscript in his briefcase and for some time showed it to no one. One of the first to read it, a former girlfriend, Clare Blanchard, told him waspishly: 'If you must publish it, for heaven's sake do it under a different name' – with hindsight one of the worst pieces of advice in literary history. Fleming claimed the writing of this 'thriller thing' had been easy, the distraction of a few hours, dashed off with 'half his brain'. He would maintain this airy attitude to the end, insisting that *Casino Royale* could be boiled down to a few key elements: 'I extracted them from my wartime memories,' he remarked, 'dolled them up, attached a hero, a villain and a heroine, and there was the book.'

This nonchalance was, we can be sure, the purest bluff, something that Fleming, as a lifelong card-player and former expert in naval intelligence, was very good at. He may have pretended to dismiss his creation, and play down its literary merit, but he must have known that he had written a remarkable book, albeit remarkably fast. The idea for Bond had been gestating in his mind, and his personality, for at least a decade. Back in 1944, as the war reached its climax, Fleming had told a friend in deep earnestness: 'I am going to write the spy story to end all spy stories.'

And that is exactly what he did.

002

THE LIFE:
SMELLING BATTLE FROM AFAR

The Life: Smelling Battle From Afar

Ian Lancaster Fleming: even his name had an imagined romance sewn into it, for his mother liked to claim descent from John of Gaunt, the fourteenth-century Duke of Lancaster and the rich and powerful son of Edward III. Whether this claim to medieval royal ancestry contained any truth is unclear, and perhaps unimportant, for Fleming family myth was a powerful force, and an important element in the genetic recipe that made up James Bond.

The Flemings were certainly wealthy and well connected. On the eve of Ian's birth, they represented the epitome of the Edwardian moneyed class, though the money was new – barely two generations old – a fact that may explain Ian's eternal preoccupation with the stuff. His grandfather, Robert, born in a Dundee slum, had made a vast fortune through American railroads and other shrewd investments, with which he had built a forty-four-room Gothic mansion in

Oxfordshire, and instant respectability. The Flemings were tweedy, hearty, thrifty and vigorous, dedicated to outdoor pursuits and blood sports. Besides money and social cachet, Robert Fleming bequeathed to his sons, including the eldest, Valentine (Ian's father), a taste for hard work, a certain Presbyterian rigidity, and a family motto that emphasised action over reflection: 'Let the deed *shaw* [show].'

Ian Fleming's parents might have stepped straight from a sepia photograph illustrating the twilight of the Edwardian era in all its doomed romance. Val Fleming was a rising star in the Conservative Party, a friend of Winston Churchill and a pillar of the landed squirearchy. A pure product of Eton and Oxford, he was handsome, gentle, intelligent and seemingly marked for success. His wife, Eve Ste Croix Rose, was equally beautiful, but bohemian, socially ambitious, wilful and artistic, with a domineering personality.

Ian, their second son, was born, on 28 May 1908, into a world of great privilege and great expectations. The first eight years of his life were idyllic, his main hurdle being how to make an impression beneath the shadow of his elder brother Peter, who was, in almost every respect, the sort of ideal child every parent longs for, and younger brothers traditionally detest. Peter was precocious, effortlessly brilliant and, if you happened to be a brother a year younger, a focus of rapt hero-worship and a permanent reminder of inadequacy. Two more brothers followed, Richard and Michael. A friend described the self-confident Fleming sons as an intimidating, charmed unit of 'strong, handsome, black-haired, blue-eyed boys'. There were the traditional nannies, and the traditionally brutal prep school, Durnford, an institution near Swanage which epitomised the strange British faith in bad food, plenty of Latin and beating from an early age. 'My coff has grown to whoping coff now,' Ian wrote to his mother stoically, at the age of seven. 'Please dont tell Mister Pellatt [the headmaster] cause just this morning he said that nun of us had coffs. I am afraid I do not like school very much.' In fact the regime seems to have made Ian no more miserable or ill than anyone else. The headmaster's wife read to the pupils from contemporary classics of boys' adventure: John Buchan's Richard Hannay stories, Fu Man Chu, *The Prisoner of Zenda* and later Bulldog Drummond, tales of strange and evil foreigners, stiff upper lips, and knock-out upper-cuts. This was the sort of story Fleming loved and, many years later, would write in an updated form.

But long before that, Fleming would find a real-life action hero tragically close to home. In 1914, Valentine Fleming had headed to the Western Front as an officer with the Oxfordshire Hussars. His moving letters to a friend and fellow officer, Winston Churchill, describing the pitted and charred landscape of the battlefront, suggest that the literary skills of both Peter and Ian were at least partly inherited. In May 1917, after a war of distinguished gallantry, Major Valentine Fleming, DSO, was killed in the trenches by shellfire.

The Fleming boys idolised their father (nicknamed 'Mokie', on account of his 'Smokey' pipe), and after his death he became an unattainable symbol of chivalry and moral goodness. In their nightly prayers, the boys would entreat the Almighty to 'Make me more like Mokie.' The desire to emulate this military father-hero would run through the lives of every Fleming son, but perhaps most notably in Ian, and his fictional counterpart. It does not do to over-psychoanalyse James Bond, but perhaps this tragedy offers some clue to 007's fatherless reverence for 'M', to the way that every villain lectures Bond as if speaking to a wayward little boy, and to the exaggerated respect Fleming showed towards older men for the rest of his life. Churchill himself wrote an obituary of Val Fleming, mourning the death of this bright hope with such a 'lovable and charming personality', and a signed, framed copy of the eulogy was kept by Ian Fleming as a treasure throughout his life. 'He was a man of thoughtful and tolerant opinions, which were not the less strongly or clearly held because they were not loudly or frequently asserted.'

Fleming would always retain what he called a 'mysterious affection' for Eton, the elite British public school he attended from 1921. Peter had, of course, preceded him, blazing a trail of athletic and academic success that Ian veered away from with all the energy and wilfulness a second son could muster. Ian was often in trouble, frequently beaten by his sadistic housemaster, and notably deficient in most aspects of his schoolwork. He also discovered girls, and lost his virginity in a box at the Royalty Kinema, Windsor – an experience that he would echo in *The Spy Who Loved Me* when describing the early love life of his heroine Vivienne Michel. Only on the athletics field did he show any real application, becoming *Victor Ludorum*, or school sports champion. Fleming was so proud of this achievement that he referred to it, wryly, in the revealing jacket blurb for *Casino Royale*: 'Like his brother Peter – a more famous author – he was sent to Eton, where he was *Victor Ludorum* two years in succession, a distinction only once equalled – presumably by another second son trying to compensate for a brilliant older brother.'

In the premature obituary provided by M in *You Only Live Twice*, we learn that James Bond was expelled from Eton, after a 'brief and undistinguished' school career following 'some alleged trouble with one of the boys' maids', and was then sent to Fettes (the Eton equivalent in Scotland). Fleming escaped a similar fate when he was removed from Eton by his mother at the age of seventeen, a term early, sent to a tutorial crammer to prepare for the army entrance exams, and then duly crammed into the Royal Military Academy at Sandhurst, the training college for army officers.

By turns truculent and romantic, Fleming was not cut out for the regimented life of a Sandhurst cadet. His tutor, however, predicted that he would probably make a good soldier, 'provided always that the Ladies don't ruin him'. It was a prophetic remark. During one of his many forays outside the barracks, Fleming conceived a passion for Peggy Barnard, the attractive daughter of a colonel. On the evening of Sandhurst Sports Day, this blameless girl had agreed to attend an Oxford ball with another man, a date that so irritated Ian that he vowed, if she went ahead with it, to go to London and 'find myself a tart'. Peggy went to the ball, and Ian went to the Forty-Three Club in Soho, carried out his threat, and came down with a nasty dose of gonorrhoea. Fleming's enraged mother booked him into a nursing home, told the Sandhurst authorities that he was ill, and then pulled him out of the college altogether. In a last-ditch effort to instil some sort of balance in her increasingly wayward son (and if possible prepare him for the Foreign Office exams, her newest ambition for him), 'Mrs Val', as she was known, dispatched Ian to a finishing school, the Tennerhof, at Kitzbühel in the Austrian Alps.

The Tennerhof was a peculiar establishment, run by an eccentric English couple, Ernan and Phyllis Forbes Dennis, a former diplomat-spy and his novelist wife. Ian learned to ski, and spent much of his time conducting brief liaisons with the local girls. 'Technique in bed is important,' he wrote in a notebook, with somewhat unattractive languor. 'It is the scornful coupling that makes the affairs of Austrians and Anglo-Saxons so fragmentary and in the end so distasteful.' Far more important than brushing up his technique in bed and on the slopes, under the indulgent care of the Forbes Dennises, Fleming would begin to read, voraciously, and start to write, tentatively. Every evening, wild-haired Phyllis Forbes Dennis would spin fantastic stories at the dinner table (having spent the early part of each day in bed writing novels under a pseudonym), and she encouraged her pupils to do likewise. Many years later, Fleming would credit Phyllis with helping to launch his career as a writer, though it would take many more years for that talent to emerge. He wrote several poems and short stories, which were vivid and expressive if rather over-cooked.

In Fleming's memory, Kitzbühel was a 'golden time', and it was followed by two more years away from England, first in Munich and then Geneva. The young Englishman cut a dashing figure: he drove a smart black two-seater Buick, developed an excellent command of French and German, and enjoyed himself thoroughly. He also became engaged, briefly, to a young Swiss woman named Monique Panchaud de Bottomes, until his mother intervened. In 1931 he took the Foreign Office exams, but did not win a place. Young Fleming had successively failed to live up to expectations at Eton and Sandhurst, and now in his bid to join the Foreign Service.

At the age of twenty-one, Fleming was handsome in a somewhat vulpine way. A broken nose (acquired in a collision on the Eton football field with Henry Douglas-Home, brother of the future Prime Minister) added to his rakish allure. Here, then, was a man of athletic good looks and Scottish ancestry, dangerous to women, cultured and charming, with a taste for fast cars, expensive things and foreign adventures. His time at Eton had been an unmitigated failure, but he could ski beautifully, speak German fluently, and seduce effortlessly. Ernan Forbes Dennis said of his young pupil: 'He has excellent taste . . . and a desire both for truth and knowledge. He is virile and ambitious, generous and kind-hearted.' There was also something solitary and reserved about his character, a central hardness. All these things could be said of the young Fleming; in time, they would also be true of James Bond.

Mrs Val stepped in once more. Ian, she decreed, would become a journalist. Strings were pulled, and in October 1931 he took paid employment for the first time at Reuters news agency. This would prove a crucial formative experience. 'I learned to write fast, and above all, be accurate,' he recalled. 'In Reuters if you weren't accurate you were fired, and that was the end of that.' Accuracy, speed and facts – the more colourful the better – these were the three key elements of a technique that would come to fruition with the Bond books. In addition, journalism would introduce Fleming to the wider world of international politics and foreign travel, the background for what was to come. In his first year in the job, Fleming covered the Alpine motor trials, an assignment that confirmed a growing fascination with fast cars, motor-racing and the associated high life, plus a Stalinist show trial of six British engineers accused of spying. Fleming's first taste of Moscow – gloomy, oppressive, granite-faced Communism – would inform his later images of Russian strength and menace. He loved it. With the chutzpah of youth, he formally requested an interview with Stalin; he was not surprised to be turned down, but was entirely astonished to received a note apparently signed by Stalin himself, explaining that he was simply too busy. The writer William Plomer, who met Fleming at this time, described him as 'like a mettlesome young horse' with 'a promise of something dashing and daring'. He seemed, thought Plomer, to 'smell some battle from afar'.

Having found a job he was good at, and enjoyed, Fleming promptly abandoned journalism for an exceptionally boring job in the City. The decision was perhaps less peculiar than it first seems. Robert Fleming had died, leaving nothing to his grandsons, whom he expected to be provided for by their father's estate. The nature of Val's will, however, meant that they would not inherit anything unless or until their mother remarried, or died. Such wills were not uncommon at the time, but it had a profound and unintended effect on Val's sons. The Fleming boys had been born to a world of money; the only problem was that they did not have very much of it. Ian Fleming, not for the last time in his life, decided to choose the more lucrative option and joined the merchant bank Cull & Co.

Fleming was not a good banker and soon shifted to

stockbroking, to which he was even less suited. Indeed, one friend described him as 'the world's worst stockbroker'. His plan was simply to 'make a packet and then get out' – an ambition often stated by financial folk that seldom comes to pass, and even more rarely produces satisfaction. Fleming spent money as fast as he made it, on golf, cards, books (he would become an avid bibliophile) and women: young women from the cocktail party circuit, including a 'rather spiffing' nightclub dancer (or 'bubble girl') called Storm, but also older women – these older women were often intelligent, with strong personalities, and by no means naive poppets or stereotypical Bond Girls; they also tended to be married, usually to people Fleming knew. Whereas Bond goes to bed with a particular type (and shape) of woman, Fleming was more catholic and perhaps less choosy in his tastes. As one girlfriend remarked, 'For Ian, women were like fishcakes. Mind you he was very fond of fishcakes, but he never pretended there was any mystique about eating them.' Bond dines on caviar and the finest fillet steak, and then sleeps with the most beautiful women; Fleming, sexually speaking, 'ate fishcakes', lots of them. He was not quite a cad, but he was certainly a lothario, a ladies' man, yet one who preferred the easy, undemanding company of fellow clubmen. He bought a former Baptist chapel in Ebury Street, Belgravia, where the British fascist leader Sir Oswald Mosley had lived, and painted the inside suit-grey. Fleming's distinctive interior decor no doubt reinforced the seductive, melancholy image that many women found irresistible, but it also reflected an innate sense of style and a fascination with colour and composition (perhaps inherited from his fashionable mother) that would find expression in his writing: room interiors are often meticulously described in the books. In upper-class party circles he was known as 'Glamour Boy', and there is no evidence he ever objected to the nickname. 'London has got its claws into me,' he told Ernan Forbes Dennis. But Fleming also got his claws into London, living a life in the capital's clubs and fleshpots of unalloyed pleasure that was expensive, pleasant, louche and intellectually unchallenging.

For millions, the Second World War was a trial or a tragedy. For a certain sort of Englishman, however, it was dangerous and thrilling, an opportunity for excitement and fulfilment in a moral cause. Many looked back on the war years, despite the deprivation, fear and violence, as a formative experience that changed for ever their perception of the world and its possibilities. For Ian Fleming, the outbreak of war was, in retrospect, a godsend. Photographs taken before the war show a young blade with hooded lids and a cruel upper lip, running to seed at speed. From 1939 onwards, he was a man with a mission: specifically, naval intelligence and espionage.

Quite how Fleming came by this mission is a small mystery. The clubland he inhabited had its share of spies, and he knew many men operating in that shadowland: Forbes Dennis had been a spy. While in Kitzbühel, Fleming had encountered Conrad O'Brien-Ffrench, a semi-independent operative in one of the shadowy spy networks, gathering information on German troop concentrations. His elder brother Peter had already begun to work for British military intelligence before the war. Some thought Ian had done likewise. In 1939, he obtained a leave of absence from his stockbroking firm in order to cover a British trade mission to Moscow as a special freelance correspondent for *The Times*. Sefton Delmer, another journalist reporting on the trade delegation, was convinced that the *Times* job was simply Ian's cover for more secret activities. Delmer had himself been employed by British intelligence as the *Daily Express* correspondent in Berlin, and would go on to work with Fleming on 'black propaganda' during the war. On his return, Fleming wrote a report on Soviet politics, an annotated and revised version of an article *The Times* had declined to publish, which found its way to various Soviet experts at the Foreign Office: 'Russia would be an exceedingly treacherous ally,' Fleming warned. And he was almost certainly debriefed by MI6, the external arm of the British secret service, on his return from his earlier Moscow visit in 1933.

Fleming was clearly attracted to the spy world. For some time before the outbreak of war, he had been providing titbits of intelligence gleaned during his skiing trips and part-time journalism. It is almost equally certain that these offerings were uninvited and, at least in some quarters, unwelcome and unappreciated. The military attaché in Berlin dismissed Fleming's early intelligence-gathering efforts as 'gullible and of poor and imbalanced judgment'. Perhaps he had been actively recruited by British intelligence at some point in the 1930s, but if so, it seems likely that Fleming would have revealed as much in the end: like many people involved in espionage, he was not very good at keeping secrets. More probably, his well-connected mother told Montagu Norman, then Governor of the Bank of England, that her son was looking for an interesting war job, and Norman gave a nod to the right channels.

According to the old saw, anyone who asks to be a spy cannot be a spy. However it came about – whether through formal or informal contact, the old spy network, the old boy network or family clout – Ian Fleming was living proof that if you really wanted to join the espionage and intelligence club, you could. On 24 May 1939, just four months before the declaration of war, Fleming sat down to lunch at the Carlton Grill with Rear Admiral John Henry Godfrey, the hard-driving Director of Naval Intelligence (DNI) and the man responsible for gathering intelligence in all areas of the war related to British naval interests – in other words, just about everywhere. Godfrey, himself barely three months into the job, had put out the word that he needed an assistant. Fleming, he decided, would be the ideal candidate.

As, indeed, he was. To date, Fleming's combination of imagination, intelligence and charm had found no more useful outlet than half-hearted money-making and full-hearted self-indulgence. He would make a superb aide to the Director of Naval Intelligence: his ability to get on with most people, particularly older, self-important men, made him the perfect liaison between the irascible Godfrey and the other parts of the British intelligence machine; his as yet unrealised literary skills lent him the resourceful thinking and imagination that is essential to effective espionage; his gambler's instinct, his taste for adventure and his ability to read personality would all be honed and developed as the feckless bon viveur was transformed into Fleming of Naval Intelligence, a pivotal operative in Britain's secret war at sea. Much of Fleming's success was a consequence of his relationship with Godfrey: the admiral was M to Fleming's Bond – an uncompromising, precise, short-tempered and loyal older man, faced with a young, gifted and unorthodox assistant, to whom he granted extraordinary licence. Years later, Godfrey, noting Fleming's 'marked flair' for intelligence planning, would pay extravagant (and perhaps excessive) tribute to his protégé: 'Ian should have been DNI and I his naval adviser.' Reflecting years later on the inspiration for Bond, Fleming was precise: 'My job got me right to the heart of things.'

The Naval Intelligence Division (NID), operating out of Rooms 38 and 39 of the Admiralty, in Whitehall, was responsible for collecting, analysing and distributing intelligence for the Admiralty, and providing security and counter-intelligence to the Royal Navy for the war at sea. But its role was far wider than this suggests, just as Fleming was far more than merely an assistant to its boss. With two thousand personnel at its peak, and through a worldwide network of agents and attachés, NID assembled a vast amount of detailed information, but also formulated active deception plans and played an important part in the complex, fast-moving and dangerous game that is wartime espionage. In addition to signals intelligence and tracking U-boats and shipping, NID helped to run agents and double agents, and dealt in stolen documents, aerial photography, coastal surveillance and numerous 'special operations' against the Germans.

In the smoky hive of Room 39, Fleming was Godfrey's front man, and as such he operated with considerable freedom: he liaised with MI6 and SOE (responsible for sabotage and subversion); he worked with the Political Warfare Executive on propaganda, and handled the press; he fielded demands for information from above, and shielded Godfrey from interference from below. 'I shared all secrets with him,' Godfrey later wrote. Fleming was also allowed to evolve and manage his own plans, or 'plots', as he referred to them – the choice of word, given his later career as a novelist, seems significant. Some of Fleming's ideas were run-of-the-mill, some were fantastical and impractical, and some, in the opinion of his colleagues, were simply mad. Even Godfrey noted that Fleming tended not to let practicalities get in the way of a good 'plot': 'He had plenty of ideas and was anxious to carry them out but was not interested in, and would prefer to ignore, the extent of the logistics background inseparable to all projects.' In a sense, Fleming's task was to dream up espionage plans with convincing scenarios; others would then be charged with trying to turn fiction into reality. In this, he was preparing for, and precisely reversing, the process that would lead to the creation of James Bond.

Among Fleming's more remarkable ideas were: scuttling cement barges in the Danube at its most narrow point in order to block the waterway for German shipping; forging Reichsmarks to disrupt the German economy; dropping an observer (possibly Fleming himself) on the island of Heligoland to monitor the shipping outside Kiel; sinking a lump of concrete off Dieppe with men inside it to observe the German coastal defences; luring German secret agents to Monte Carlo and capturing them; and floating a radio ship in the North Sea to broadcast depressing and/or irritating propaganda to the Germans. 'What nonsense they were,' Fleming would later write, 'those romantic Red Indian daydreams so many of us indulged in at the beginning of the war.' They may have seemed nonsensical in retrospect, but at the time they were matters of life and death, and Ian treated his new job with a dedication he had never shown before, starting work at 6 a.m. and continuing late into the night. 'It was deadly serious as well as intellectually stimulating,' wrote one colleague. Lieutenant Fleming received wartime promotions to acting lieutenant commander in the Royal Naval Volunteer Reserve, then acting commander – the same rank as James Bond.

'Operation Ruthless', which Fleming concocted in September 1940, offers an excellent example of his talents as both an espionage planner and a novelist. The cryptanalysts at Bletchley Park had already broken the code used on the fabled Enigma machine by the German Abwehr, or military intelligence service, but they had not yet penetrated the mysteries of the code used by the German navy, which used a different coding machine. NID wanted a codebook, so Fleming came up with a plan. The Germans had begun operating a rescue boat in the English Channel to pick up downed pilots. If this boat, presumably carrying a codebook aboard, could be lured to pick up what looked like a downed German plane, the crew could be overpowered and the codebook seized. Fleming's plan came in three acts:

Obtain from the Air Ministry an air-worthy German bomber. Pick a tough crew of five, including pilot, W/T (wireless/telegraph) officer and word-perfect German speaker. Dress them in German Air Force uniforms, add blood and bandages to suit.

Crash plane in the Channel after making SOS to rescue service.

Once aboard rescue boat, shoot German crew, dump
overboard, bring rescue boat back to English port.

Fleming added a Bond touch, insisting that the pilot be a
'tough bachelor, able to swim'. A Heinkel He 111 bomber,
shot down over Scotland and since repaired, was obtained,
along with some German uniforms. The plan sounded simple,
but, as with many Fleming plots, there were serious practical
objections, not least the argument that a Heinkel crashed at
speed might kill its crew on impact or sink so fast that all
inside would drown. Undaunted, Ian proposed to accompany
the crew in person, an idea that was flatly rejected by Godfrey:
'Ian was someone who simply could not fall into enemy hands
because he was privy to everything.' To Fleming's chagrin,
'Operation Ruthless' was first postponed and then abandoned.

Despite such setbacks, Commander Fleming was not
content to spend the war pushing paper from behind a desk,
no matter how interesting the paper or how imposing the
desk. In June 1940, Fleming apparently flew to Paris as
France was collapsing under the German onslaught. There
he is said to have extracted a large sum of money from the
safe at the Rolls-Royce headquarters in Paris where MI6
kept its funds, before heading south to make contact with
Admiral Jean-François Darlan, head of the French navy.
Britain needed to know whether Darlan would come over
to the British side, or whether his fleet might fall into German
hands. Godfrey wanted Fleming to find out.

When Fleming arrived, Bordeaux was in chaos, teeming with refugees. The newly arrived naval lieutenant commander helped with evacuation, burned most of the papers at the British Consulate, and using a simple line of argument persuaded a number of French merchant vessels to help with the evacuation: 'If you don't take these people on board and transport them to England, I can promise you that if the Germans don't sink you, the Royal Air Force will.' Fleming made his way home via Madrid and Portugal, but before leaving France he came up with a typically imaginative suggestion for dealing with Darlan and the French fleet: 'Why doesn't His Majesty's government offer Admiral Darlan the Isle of Wight for the duration of the war, and make it French territory under the French flag for the entire period?' The suggestion, needless to say, was not taken up; instead, the British, unwilling to take any further chances with Darlan's promises, shelled and torpedoed the French fleet at Mers-el-Kébir to prevent the Germans from getting their hands on it. Fleming reflected ruefully that perhaps he should 'leave the conduct of the war to older and conceivably wiser heads'. Conceivably, but then again, Fleming's idea might have saved 1,250 French lives, removed a source of French animosity that lingers to this day, and changed the course of the war. How the residents of the Isle of Wight would have felt to discover that they had suddenly become French can only be imagined.

One of Fleming's most notable contributions to wartime

intelligence was the creation of 30 Assault Unit (30 AU), a commando group dedicated to gathering intelligence in advance of the main British fighting force. Fleming and Bond expert Henry Chancellor has described 30 AU as 'in effect, the private army of the Naval Intelligence Department'; if so, then Fleming was its general, though never in the field. He referred to them as his 'Red Indians' – somewhat to their annoyance, since a number of these warriors had little time for their self-styled chief. Recruited from other commando units, the men of 30 AU, which was initially only thirty strong but eventually more than five times that size, were trained in unarmed combat, safe-cracking, code-breaking and other nefarious arts. A similar force had been deployed by the Germans to capture Allied documents, codes and equipment; Fleming considered it 'one of the most outstanding innovations in German intelligence' and worked hard to copy it. Inevitably, 30 AU attracted men of a particular stamp: daring, independent-minded buccaneers, stylish in a brutal way and supremely tough. One member of the unit described them as 'fairly piratical, especially with the women'. These 'tough commando types', as Fleming remembered them, would form the bedrock of James Bond's character.

Some men of what would become 30 AU got their first taste of action during the disastrous Dieppe raid of August 1942, the major assault launched by six thousand British and Canadian troops to test the German defences on the northern coast of France. Fleming was allowed to accompany a Royal

Marine Commando unit, but only as an observer. He watched the raid unfold from the deck of HMS *Fernie*, a Hunt-class destroyer eight hundred yards offshore, while the men of the unit waited to go ashore from a nearby gunboat. Fleming wrote a vivid account of the calamity, the confusion and, above all, the horrible cacophony, as the Allied attackers were pinned down by machine-gun fire, with the Canadian troops suffering particularly heavy losses. By mid-morning it had become clear that the unit was never going to be able to disembark from HMS *Locust* and reach the beach, and as the shattered raiding party prepared to withdraw, a shell struck HMS *Fernie*, killing one crewman and wounding several others. Fleming was happy enough when the captain of HMS *Fernie* decided the time had come to head home. He would later write sardonically: 'I had been instructed to return to England independently directly a certain mission had been accomplished, and when it was clear that the gunboat was not going to be able to carry out her original instructions, the Government exhortation "Is Your Journey Really Necessary?" came to my mind, heavily underlined by the shells from the shore batteries which came zipping through our rigging.'

Some three thousand British and Canadian troops were killed or captured in the Dieppe raid. This was the closest Ian Fleming would ever get to real war. His sister-in-law, the actress Celia Johnson, married to Peter, noted that this brief encounter with death had shaken even Ian's capacity for understatement. It seemed, she said, as if 'he had his breath taken away once or twice'. Fleming's ironic tone does not exactly suggest a man itching for battle, but then opinion was (and remains) divided over whether Ian was simply an armchair warrior or a genuine warrior confined to an armchair against his will by the nature of his job. Edward Merrett, who shared Room 39 with Fleming in those years, dismissed the notion that his former colleague was keen to get to grips with the enemy, a danger-loving James Bond *manqué*. 'He was a pen-pusher, like all of us,' said Merrett. 'If he was secretly longing for action I never saw any sign of it.' But another colleague, Peter Smithers, may have been closer to the mark when he speculated that Ian's creative urges sprang directly from having to imagine scenes of adventure and espionage, without actually witnessing the events in person. 'Ian constantly longed to be personally engaged in the excitement. He was of an essentially aggressive nature. It was the repression of these desires by authority, quite rightly, which in my opinion fired the imagination engaged in his books.' In the books, Fleming hints at Bond's heroic wartime service, recording that he saw action in the Ardennes forest in 1944, operated 'behind enemy lines', and killed two enemy agents during the war – a Japanese code-breaker at the Rockefeller Center in New York and a Norwegian double agent whom he stabs to death in Stockholm. Whether Ian Fleming would have liked to play a similarly dramatic part in the war is moot. John Godfrey was not about to allow him to head off to places where he might be killed: Fleming was simply too useful where he was, and, as 'the only officer who had a finger in practically every pie', he knew too much to risk being captured.

In the Bond novels, 007 is described as having spent much of the war travelling the world on various missions. That was certainly Fleming's lucky experience. Operation Golden Eye was the back-up plan to maintain communication with Gibraltar and launch sabotage operations in case the Nazis invaded Spain; setting up the plan, which never had to be used, took Fleming to Spain, Portugal, Tangiers and Gibraltar itself. It would also of course become the name of his Jamaican home. Fleming found himself in close contact with intelligence operatives in the United States, most notably the Canadian William Stephenson, head of British intelligence in North America, and William 'Big Bill' Donovan, the lawyer, First World War veteran and US government official who would play a crucial role in Anglo-American intelligence and the creation of the Office of Strategic Services (OSS), which would later evolve into the CIA.

In May 1941, Fleming accompanied Godfrey to the States, ostensibly to inspect security in US ports, but also to help William Stephenson and Donovan develop the intelligence relationship with America. On the way, they stopped at Estoril, near Lisbon, where Fleming gambled at the casino with some Portuguese businessmen, and lost. On leaving,

Fleming remarked: 'What if those men had been German secret service agents, and suppose we had cleaned them out of their money; now that would have been exciting.' It was another glimpse into the workings of Fleming's imagination. The scene would marinade in his mind for a decade before finding its way into the most memorable moment in *Casino Royale*, when Bond cleans out the repulsive communist agent Le Chiffre.

In Washington, Godfrey and Fleming met J. Edgar Hoover, the head of the FBI, for exactly sixteen minutes, but soon afterwards Roosevelt followed British advice and made Bill Donovan head of the new government intelligence department that would later become the OSS. At Donovan's request, Fleming penned a seventy-page memo with suggestions on the shape a US intelligence agency should take after the war. His description of the ideal secret agent has the unmistakable ring of Bond: 'must have trained powers of observation, analysis and evaluation; absolute discretion, sobriety, devotion to duty; language and wide experience, and be aged about 40 to 50'. Fleming would later claim, not entirely seriously, that this work had been instrumental in forming the CIA charter; even if this was not strictly true, Donovan was grateful enough to present Fleming with a .38 Colt revolver inscribed 'For Special Services'. In later life, Fleming would stoke speculation by declining to say exactly what these services had been, while hinting that they had been very special indeed.

Fleming made two more trips across the Atlantic, for conferences at which Churchill and Roosevelt discussed Allied strategy. The second, in Quebec in 1943, involved one of the odder moments in the Fleming–Bond biography. Bill Stephenson, the mastermind behind British intelligence in North America, would later claim that during this visit Fleming attended Camp X, the notoriously tough training centre near Toronto where SOE and OSS agents were put through their paces. More than that, Stephenson claimed that Fleming had excelled at the course, including unarmed combat, placing a fake bomb in a Toronto power station, swimming underwater to an offshore tanker and attaching a limpet mine to the hull (strongly reminiscent of a scene in *Live and Let Die*), and firing a Sten gun on the rifle range with 'extraordinary relish'. Most bizarrely, at the end of the course, each trainee was supposedly issued with a revolver and told to kill a man at a specific address. According to Stephenson, this was the only aspect of the course Fleming flunked; he would later declare that he 'could never kill a man in that way'.

However, the historian of Camp X, David Stafford, could find no evidence that Ian Fleming had ever attended a course there. The courses described by Stephenson, at which his friend supposedly excelled, were not on the curriculum. It is certainly possible, even likely, that he visited the camp in 1943; he may even have taken part in a few training events. But the notion that Fleming outperformed the real spies at the most demanding of all wartime spy camps is pure fiction, and soon would be.

Despite the sudden sacking of Admiral Godfrey in December 1942, as the war headed to its finale, Ian continued to play a prominent role in naval intelligence. His travels continued, including a round-the-world trip to coordinate intelligence for the new British Pacific Fleet that took him to Cairo, Ceylon, Australia and then home via Pearl Harbor. He also visited Jamaica to attend a conference on the U-boat threat in the Caribbean, and fell in love with the island. Here he would build his holiday home, Goldeneye, and here he would, in time, write every one of the Bond novels.

In March 1944, Fleming was charged with running the committee which channelled top-secret information to the Royal Navy units preparing to invade Normandy. The 'Red Indians', 30 AU, would be part of the attack, and Fleming compiled lists of the sort of information and equipment to be scooped up ahead of the invasion force. As the German army retreated, 30 AU scoured after it. Later, the unit would be the first Allied force to enter the naval port of Kiel. Fleming's 'Red Indians' picked up some astonishing technological booty: an acoustic homing torpedo hidden in a mushroom farm, an amphibious machine for exploding beach mines, and a one-man submarine – complete with decomposing crewman inside, one dead eye pressed to the periscope. At Tambach Castle, 30 AU came across the entire German naval archives dating back to 1870, under the care of three German admirals. Fleming himself travelled to Germany to ensure their safe return to Britain. As for the three admirals, according to one account, Fleming ordered that they be killed, but when the lieutenant charged with this refused, he relented. Something about this story does not ring true: whatever brutal qualities he might invest in his fictional agent, Fleming was not the killing kind.

Fleming never claimed to be James Bond. He did not have to: the critics and media did that for him. But he was careful not to deny it too forcefully either. He was only too happy to be photographed with gun in hand, and to hint at dark doings in his wartime spy days. He had travelled the world helping to spin the wartime spy web, and he had seen fighting at first hand. However, most of his war had taken place behind a London desk, dreaming up plots; his second successful career would involve the same process, but at a different desk. In later years, Fleming would refer to 'school and war and other uncivilised experiences'; in truth, his war had been a remarkably civilised affair.

After six and a half years with naval intelligence, Fleming was no longer the callow, spoiled young man he had been in 1939. He had found a world, of secret agents and espionage, of adventure, violence and intrigue, that delighted him, satisfying both his intellect and romanticism. Churchill himself asserted that 'in the higher ranges of Secret Service work, the actual facts of many cases were in every respect equal to the most fantastic inventions of romance and melodrama. Tangle within tangle, plot and counter-plot, ruse and treachery, cross and double-cross, true agent, false agent, double agent, gold and steel, the bomb, the dagger and the firing party, were interwoven in many a texture so intricate as to be incredible and yet true.' Fleming would later quote that passage with approval, having converted his own experience of the tangled world into novels. It would be another seven years before he sat down to create Bond, but much of the material was already in place. Fleming had met dangerous adventurers, and known subtle spies; in the midst of war, he had travelled to distant corners of the world; he had witnessed the remarkable power of modern gadgetry in the spy's armoury; he had seen how secret agents are made; he had watched men die; and he had held the power of life and death in his own hands. Above all, his job with naval intelligence had taken place in a wartime world where anything seemed possible. Winning a war, like writing a novel, required one weapon above all others: imagination.

Back in London in 1946, Fleming returned to journalism and accepted the post of foreign news manager of the Kemsley newspaper group, which included the *Sunday Times*, the *Empire News*, the *Sunday Graphic* and a raft of local and regional newspapers. As the former press liaison officer for NID, he had struck up a close friendship with the proprietor, Lord Kemsley, during the war, and his contract was astonishingly generous: a fat wage for an undemanding job, a large expense account and, crucially, two months off in early spring of every year to spend in Jamaica. Fleming was manager of some eighty foreign correspondents, whose locations were indicated by a map behind his desk with a number of flashing lights. These correspondents (some of whom were also spies) were hired, fired, paid and commissioned by Fleming. Over the next fourteen years, he would perform numerous roles at the *Sunday Times*: manager, columnist and writer on subjects as diverse as gambling and travel. His was an easy, pleasant and unchallenging life. Fleming's description in *Moonraker* of Bond's daily routine when not on assignment is a fairly accurate depiction of his own easygoing existence in these years: 'Elastic office hours from around ten to six, lunch . . . evenings spent playing cards in the company of a few close friends . . . or making love, with rather cold passion, to one of three similarly disposed married women, weekends playing golf for high stakes.'

But just as Bond secretly awaits the call from M, so Fleming was also preparing himself, perhaps subconsciously, for a belated call-up from his own muse: gathering material, honing his wartime memories, travelling the world, and preparing Bond's life within his own.

003

WHO WAS JAMES BOND?

Who Was James Bond?

Every acquaintance of Ian Fleming ran the risk of ending up as a character, or a characteristic, in one of his Bond books. Fleming was, like most fiction writers, an avid collector of facts: he gathered names, plots, meals, venues and words from the places he had been and the people he had met. Reality underpins the fiction: while producing the stream of Bond books, Fleming would also find time to write two books of non-fiction, on diamonds and travel, both subjects which loom large in the novels. Almost every character in his fiction is based, to some extent, on a real person, even if only by name. He plucked these names from his social circle, his memory, his reading, his favourite Jamaican newspaper, the *Daily Gleaner*, and his imagination: old school friends (and enemies), clubmen, colleagues in the City and Fleet Street, golfing partners, girlfriends and others found themselves transported into Fleming's fiction. This was all very well if you happened to be named after a heroic bit-part player or a curvaceous new lover, but several of Fleming's acquaintances were mortally offended to discover that their names had been appropriated and attached to the most fearsome fictional villains. The Bond books are not *romans-à-clef*, straightforward fictionalisations of living people, but rather careful, teasing and often witty interleavings of fact and fiction, imagined people with real names, and real people with invented names in imagined situations. Working out who's who in Bond, and who might be partially based on whom (as well as who later claimed to be whom, and probably wasn't), is one of the most intriguing and complex aspects of the relationship between Ian Fleming and James Bond.

Where did James Bond – the name – come from? As with all aspects of the Bond stories, there are several theories and a number of speculations. The most popular (and one that he publicly affirmed) is that Fleming, sitting down to work at his desk in Goldeneye, simply lifted the name from his bookshelves, his eye having alighted upon *Field Guide to Birds of the West Indies* by James Bond, the standard reference book published by Macmillan in 1947. Fleming was fascinated by wildlife, and birds in particular: 'For Your Eyes Only' opens with a detailed description of the streamer-tail or doctor hummingbird, which again may be derived from the other James Bond. In 1964, long after his name had become a global brand, the American ornithologist paid a surprise visit to Fleming in Jamaica. A Canadian film crew happened to be conducting an interview with Fleming at the time, and with a happy flourish, the author introduced his unexpected guest as 'the real James Bond'. In the film *Die Another Day*, starring Pierce Brosnan, Bond picks up a copy of *Field Guide to Birds of the West Indies* and disguises himself as an ornithologist, in elaborate homage to the origin of the name.

Though James Bond may have been christened after an expert bird-spotter plucked at random from a book spine, it is possible that the name was already stored somewhere in Fleming's mind when he began to write *Casino Royale*. During the war, C. H. Forster, a friend who was then working in the Ministry of Aircraft Production, recalled a casual conversation in which Fleming described how he planned to come up with fictional names if he wrote a book. 'That's easy,' he said. 'I think of the first couple of names in my house at school and change their Christian names.' Forster told him that the first names in *his* school register had been James Aitken and Harry Bond. 'So you could have Harry Aitken and James Bond'. Fleming had allegedly remarked that 'James Bond' sounded better. There are other possibilities. Peter Fleming knew an SIS officer named Rodney Bond, who had saved his life during a clandestine operation in Greece. According to the British diplomat Harold Caccia (who had been rescued by Rodney Bond in the same operation), when Ian Fleming was looking for a name for his fictional hero, it was his brother Peter who suggested he be named in honour of his wartime colleague. There is also a character named James Bond in the Agatha Christie short story 'The Rajah's Emerald', published in 1934: Fleming may have read the story, leaving the name lodged somewhere in his subconscious. Bondologists have also noted that there is a church in Toronto called St James Bond, which Fleming might conceivably have seen on his visit to Canada during the war – although his Bond, of course, is no kind of saint.

Any, all or none of these factors may have contributed to the naming of Bond. What is certain is that once he had alighted on the name, Fleming knew it fitted his spy like a Savile Row suit. 'I wanted the simplest, dullest, plainest-sounding name I could find,' he said, something 'brief, unromantic, Anglo-Saxon and yet very masculine.' A name like 'Peregrine Maltravers', he reflected, would be too exotic for a man intended to be a 'neutral figure – an anonymous blunt instrument wielded by a Government Department'. What Fleming did not say is that 'Peregrine Maltravers' is also an avowedly *upper-class* English name. Scottish-born Bond, for all his clubbable ways and public school education, is intended to be classless (or as classless as an upper-class man like Fleming could make him). The bi-syllabic James Bond has a double-barrelled simplicity to it. 'Bond' sounds oddly British and reassuring: a bond is what an Englishman's word is made of, the financial security one may reliably invest in, the adhesive that holds things together. With no offence to Peregrines worldwide, this is not a name women tend to go to bed with on first acquaintance, and the phrase 'The name's Maltravers, Peregrine Maltravers' hardly trips off the tongue. In *The Man with the Golden Gun*, Bond, refusing a knighthood, reflects on his own name: 'No middle name. No hyphen. A quiet, dull, anonymous name.'

The codename 007 may have a simpler origin. One of the greatest triumphs of British naval intelligence in the First World War had been the breaking of the code in the fabled Zimmermann Telegram of 1917, which helped bring the United States into the war and effectively sealed Germany's defeat. The telegram, sent by German Foreign Minister Arthur Zimmermann, instructed the German ambassador in Mexico to approach the Mexican government with a view to forming an alliance against the US. The message was intercepted and decoded by three naval intelligence code-breakers, working out of Room 40 in the Admiralty; two months later, an outraged US Congress declared war on Germany. The German diplomatic code used in the top-secret telegram was identified by the number 0075; thereafter the double-zero code was attached to all highly classified documents. To anyone versed in intelligence history, 007 signified the highest achievement of British military espionage. 'When I was in the Admiralty during the war,' Fleming told a later interviewer, 'all the top-secret signals had the double-O prefix. Although this was later changed for security reasons, it stuck in my mind and I decided to borrow it for Bond to make his job more interesting and provide him with a licence to kill.' The sixteenth-century English mathematician, occultist and secret agent, Dr John Dee, used a similar code in messages sent to Queen Elizabeth I. In Dee's code the double-O prefix, symbolising two eyes, was shorthand for 'For Your Eyes Only'.

Like most fictional characters, James Bond is not one individual. 'He was a compound of all the secret agents and commando types I met during the war,' Fleming once declared. 'It was all the things that I heard and learned about secret operations that finally led me to write about them in a disguised way and with James Bond as the central character.' Fleming never denied that Bond was a combination of real people; he did not, however, identify exactly *which* people, leaving the door open to an entire raft of claimants. Fleming compounded the issue by flattering more than one person with the suggestion that he was the model for the super-spy; inevitably, as Bond's fame spread, this was an increasingly coveted accolade.

Chief among the contenders is, of course, Fleming himself. The physical descriptions of 007 recall his creator, with his 'longish nose' and slightly 'cruel mouth'. They even share the same colour (blue) eyes and black hair. In *From Russia with Love*, Fleming provides the most detailed picture of Bond, complete with elements of self-portraiture: 'The eyes wide and level under straight, rather long black

eyebrows . . . the line of the jaws rather straight but firm.'
In *Casino Royale*, Bond's looks remind the doomed beauty
Vesper Lynd of Hoagy Carmichael, the American songwriter,
singer and actor. The comparison is made again in *Moonraker*,
in which Bond is described as 'certainly good-looking . . .
Rather like Hoagy Carmichael in a way. That black hair
falling down over the right eyebrow. Much the same bones.
But there was something a bit cruel in the mouth, and the
eyes were cold.' An image of Bond, approved by Fleming
as part of the *Daily Express* strip cartoon that started in
1958, makes 007 appear faintly vampiric, but again bears
more than a passing resemblance to Fleming himself.
Fleming sometimes played up the autobiographical aspects
of Bond, and sometimes downplayed them: 'I couldn't
possibly be James Bond,' he told his friend, William Plomer.
'He's got more guts than I have. He's also considerably
more handsome.'

Val Fleming, the courageous father killed in the trenches
of the First World War, must have a primary claim to be
the inspiration for James Bond. The father, dead when Ian
Fleming was just eight years old, naturally left a permanent
hole in Fleming's world, which Bond may partly have filled
by representing his ideal man of action. It is possible,
though simplistic, to see Bond as an expression of father/
hero-worship played out in fiction, though Val was far too
fastidious, gentle and conventional to be confused with the
hard-eyed Bond.

Peter Fleming, Ian's much-admired elder brother, may have come a little closer to that model, being handsome, tough and, most importantly, a secret warrior. Having forged one career in peacetime as a highly successful travel writer, Peter had enjoyed an adventurous war. Drafted early into the world of military intelligence and irregular warfare, he was sent to Norway on a reconnaissance mission to plot a counter-attack following the Nazi invasion, and was erroneously reported killed. Mirroring Ian's role in naval intelligence, Peter had become assistant to the chief of military intelligence, and thus privy to some of the most delicate and fascinating secrets of wartime spying. He again narrowly escaped death while on an SOE mission to Greece, and was then transferred to Delhi, where he spent three years organising deception plans quite as elaborate as anything dreamed up by his brother. One such plot involved planting a briefcase full of forged papers in a crashed jeep in the jungle, to try to convince the advancing Japanese that they were facing an unexpectedly strong British force. After the war, Peter returned to writing and produced a novel, *The Sixth Column*, which had as its main character a thriller writer who creates a protagonist with marked similarities to Bond. In at least three ways, then, Peter helped to create Bond: by a successful writing career that may initially have put off his younger brother but later spurred him on to try his hand at fiction; by a wartime intelligence career with some enviably Bond-like aspects; and by writing a book that uncannily prefigured

Ian's own literary career. Just six months after Peter published *The Sixth Column*, Ian set to work on *Casino Royale*.

Behind the Flemings follow a parade of swashbuckling types, each with a claim to a little of the Bond myth. One of the earliest is Conrad O'Brien-Ffrench, the skiing spy Fleming had first met in Kitzbühel back in the 1930s, when the older man was gathering information on German troop deployments as part of the Z Organisation, an amateur spy network made up of journalists and businessmen. While Fleming certainly met and admired this extraordinary character, he is unlikely to have known about his espionage activities in enough detail to use them as material in the Bond series.

A more likely candidate is Patrick Dalzel-Job, who served in the 30 AU unit during the latter part of the war. Dalzel-Job displayed many of Bond's characteristics: he was a superb marksman who had learned how to ski backwards, parachute behind enemy lines, dive, and pilot a miniature submarine. When on assignment, he wore an airman's jacket with a compass hidden inside one of the buttons and carried a pipe with a hidden chamber containing maps. Jan Aylen, technical officer with 30 AU, declared Dalzel-Job to be 'one of the most enterprising, plucky and resourceful' warriors he had ever met. Like Fleming, Dalzel-Job had lost his father in the trenches, and spent much of his youth navigating around the Norwegian coast with his mother, gaining a specialist knowledge that proved invaluable when war was declared and he signed up with British Naval Intelligence. Serving with the North Western Expeditionary Force in Norway in 1940, Dalzel-Job revealed a Bond-like streak of rebellion when he disobeyed a direct order and insisted on evacuating five thousand Norwegian civilians from the town of Narvik who were facing imminent Nazi retaliation. He escaped a court martial after King Haakon of Norway awarded him the Knight's Cross of St Olav in recognition of his gallantry, 'making it difficult for me to be disciplined', in his own words.

By the time Fleming met him in 1944, Dalzel-Job had already won a reputation for bravery just this side of lunacy, which continued to expand in the closing months of the war. Striking out from Utah Beach after the D-Day landings with a handful of Royal Marines, he filleted vital intelligence from an abandoned flying-bomb site, disabled a German destroyer and personally accepted the surrender of the German city of Bremen. He then immediately set off on a quixotic quest to find the Norwegian woman who had once served as crew on his boat, and married her three weeks later.

Throughout his long life, Dalzel-Job, who died in 2003 at the age of ninety, was credited with being the model for James Bond. He never denied the association, and claimed that Fleming had told him, long after the war, that he was indeed an inspiration for Bond. But disarmingly, this diminutive figure with large ears who lived in retirement in the Scottish Highlands pointed out that in certain respects he was no Bond: 'I have never read a Bond book or seen a Bond movie. They are not my style . . . And I only ever loved one woman, and I'm not a drinking man.' Yet he also implied that he knew what was in the books and films, and recognised himself. 'When you have lived such an exciting life you don't need to see a fictional account of it,' he said, adding, perhaps unnecessarily, since he was approaching the age of eighty-seven: 'I prefer the quiet life now.' It is possible that the villain Oddjob in *Goldfinger* may be a sly joke on the name Dalzel-Job.

Dalzel-Job may have the strongest claim to be Bond, but he was not the only prototype among the ranks of hard men in naval special operations. Another was Michael Mason, the scion of a landed Oxfordshire family who ran away to become a fur-trapper in rural Canada and then enjoyed a second career as a successful amateur boxer. At the outbreak of war, the rugged Mason was operating as an agent in Romania when two Nazi agents were sent to assassinate him; he killed them both. Another with a claim to a bit of Bond was the extraordinary Merlin Minshall, an amateur racing driver who took part in Fleming's abortive attempt to disrupt traffic on the Danube by scuttling six cement barges at the river's narrowest point, the Iron Gates. Minshall, who had spent much of his life sailing the waterways of Europe, simply walked into Room 39 in 1939 and suggested the idea off his own bat. Minshall was sent to Bucharest in 1940 with orders to help Mason carry out the scheme. The cement barges were duly chartered and headed up the Danube to the Iron Gates, with Minshall following behind in a high-speed launch. Everything went wrong: the launch ran out of fuel, the plan was betrayed and the local Nazis appeared. In true Bond tradition, Minshall then set off in the launch and escaped, it is said, after a two-hour high-speed chase. Minshall, who spent the latter part of the war tracking U-boats and worked as naval liaison to Tito's partisans in Yugoslavia, was one of the first to claim consanguinity with Bond.

A similar man of action was Fitzroy Maclean, the diplomat, writer and adventurer who carried out covert operations behind the lines in North Africa as part of the newly formed SAS, and later played a pivotal role liaising with Tito's partisans in Yugoslavia. In 1942, he abducted at gunpoint a Nazi sympathiser in Persia, General Zahidi, and spirited him out of the country. Fleming first met Maclean in Moscow in 1939, when he was on special assignment for *The Times*. Maclean, then serving as a junior diplomat at the Moscow embassy, was sent to summon Fleming to a dinner and found him in flagrante delicto in his hotel room with an attractive Russian woman (who turned out to be a Soviet plant, sent to spy on the journalist). Maclean told the dinner party hostess that Fleming could not attend as he was 'very, very busy'. Despite their shared interests, the friendship between the two men appears to have cooled after the war. Fleming later considered Maclean's superb book *Eastern Approaches* for serialisation in the *Sunday Times*, then rejected it rather pointedly, insisting that the author had claimed too much credit for himself – something Fleming would surely not have done had Maclean been the inspiration for Bond.

The playboy double agent Dušan 'Duško' Popov, code-named 'Tricycle' by the British, is yet another individual cited as a proto-Bond: certainly he shared many of Bond's (and for that matter Fleming's) tastes, including casinos, women, fast cars, expensive clothes and strong drink. Throughout the war, in the guise of an international busi-nessman, Popov fed MI5-supplied disinformation to the German Abwehr, which continued to regard (and pay) him as one of its best spies. Fleming may well have known of Tricycle's exploits, but it is highly unlikely that they ever met. In one celebrated incident, Popov was gambling in Lisbon when he became irritated by the attitude of a large and vulgar Lithuanian, who kept showing off by calling '*Banque ouverte!*' whenever he held the bank, to indicate there was no upper limit on the stakes. Popov slapped $30,000 on the table – money which belonged to MI5. The Lithuanian, eyes bulging, declined the bet. Having success-fully called his bluff, Popov tucked the money back in his dinner jacket and walked out. The incident became part of the Popov legend, and may have formed part of the inspiration for the gambling scenes in *Casino Royale*. Louche, charming and insufferably vain, Popov was a nerveless secret agent who, like Bond, never hesitated in his duty and seemed to care not one whit for the victims and wronged women he left in his wake. In later life, when asked whether he was an inspiration for James Bond, Popov managed to imply that he was more Bond than Bond himself. In 1981, he told a group of Italian journalists: 'I doubt whether a flesh and blood Bond would last forty-eight hours as a spy.'

In a similar mould was Wilfred 'Biffy' Dunderdale, the station chief of SIS (MI6) in Paris, whom Fleming met in 1940. A regular at Maxim's restaurant on the rue Royale, exquisite in Cartier cufflinks and handmade suit, and driving an armour-plated Rolls-Royce through Paris, the fashionable multilingual Dunderdale had much of Bond's style. He was also a most effective spy, having played a key role in the intelligence work that led to the cracking of the Enigma code – arguably the greatest coup in espionage history.

No account of possible Bond prototypes would be complete without mentioning William Stephenson, the Canadian spy chief codenamed 'Intrepid', who ran British intelligence in North America. We know that Fleming and Stephenson were friends and allies. Stephenson boosted the legend of Fleming as Bond, and the writer returned the compliment. In a letter to the *Sunday Times* in October 1962, Fleming declared: 'James Bond is a highly romanticised version of a true spy. The real thing is . . . William

Stephenson.' This has been taken to imply that the 'quiet Canadian' was the main inspiration for Bond, which is not exactly what Fleming was saying. Stephenson was, indeed, 'the real thing'; he was, in Fleming's own assessment, 'very tough, very rich, single-minded, patriotic and a man of few words'. He had had an extraordinary career in the First World War, during which he was gassed, learned to fly with the Royal Flying Corps, shot down Lothar von Richthofen, brother of the celebrated Red Baron, crashed, was captured and escaped. But by the second war he was middle-aged, and no longer the type to be indulging in car chases and love affairs. Working without a salary, under the official title of British Passport Control Officer, Stephenson used the so-called British Security Coordination (a front for British intelligence) to influence American opinion, channel top-secret information, and train secret agents at Camp X in Ontario. Some two thousand agents would pass through this camp during the course of the war, five of whom would go on to direct the CIA. Stephenson's plan (which never materialised) to obtain nearly three million dollars in gold belonging to the Vichy government from the Caribbean island of Martinique, may have inspired the plot of *Goldfinger*, in which the arch-villain seeks to empty Fort Knox. Stephenson's plot involved overthrowing the Vichy authorities on the island, getting the colony to declare for General de Gaulle, and then handing the gold reserves over to the Free French. Stephenson undoubtedly played a vital role in

Britain's wartime espionage and taught Fleming much of the craft he knew so well, but in many ways he is closer to M, the veteran spymaster, than to Bond himself.

There is no definitive answer to the question, who was 'the real Bond', since, as he is a fictional creation, there was no such thing. Teasing apart the claims and counterclaims is made harder by the fact that spies lie so easily, particularly when remembering their own lives. The entertaining memoirs of Popov, Minshall and Stephenson should all be taken with large quantities of salt. Bond is all of the above, and none of them: he possesses the cunning of William Stephenson, the sheer toughness of Michael Mason, the insouciant style of Popov, the disobedience of Dalzel-Job, the elegant cufflinks of Biffy Dunderdale, the courage of Merlin Minshall, and Fitzroy Maclean's intelligent heroism. Bond is all of these, but flavoured throughout with a healthy dollop of Fleming himself and his remarkable family. These intoxicating elements were then shaken up together, and stirred.

Who was M?

At first this seems a far easier question to answer, but, as with all Fleming stories, the plot is thicker than it seems. The fictional Admiral Sir Miles Messervy KCMG (finally identified by name in *The Man with the Golden Gun*) is based, in large part, on John Godfrey, Fleming's boss at the Naval

Intelligence Department. M is grumpy, dedicated, rude and every inch the naval martinet, with 'damnably clear' bright blue eyes; his underlings are terrified and loyal in equal parts. He 'thinks in the language of battleships', and his voice is straight off the Quarterdeck (the name of his house). Kingsley Amis assiduously totted up the various ways M's voice is described by Fleming: angry (3); brutal, cold (7); curt, dry (5); gruff (7); stern, testy (5); and so on. Yet this is the voice Bond 'loved and obeyed'. All these traits were apparent in Godfrey, who nonetheless ran a tight ship and proved a most effective spymaster. Fleming described him as a 'real war-winner' with 'the mind and character of a Bohemian mathematician'. Some found Godfrey impossible to deal with, and his abrupt sacking in 1942 (and lack of wartime decoration) has never been fully explained. But, like Bond, Fleming knew how to play his short-tempered boss, and was treated with similar indulgence: M lets Bond get away with, and periodically commissions him for, murder. In *On Her Majesty's Secret Service*, Fleming makes the M–Godfrey link most explicit, describing the door-knocker on M's house as the ship's bell clapper from 'HMS *Repulse*', which 'had been M's final sea-going appointment'. Godfrey's last command, before taking over at NID, had been the *Repulse*.

In a strange case of truth following fiction, Godfrey would eventually ask Fleming to write his biography (Fleming declined), yet it seems the inspiration for M was not entirely pleased to be immortalised as the boss of a cold-blooded killer, who was prepared to employ Bond to kill the crooks who had murdered his friends (in 'For Your Eyes Only'). 'He turned me into that unsavoury character, M,' Godfrey complained after Fleming's death. 'Ian wanted people to take M seriously and questioned me closely about his notional age and career. The end result did not convince or thrill.'

The use of the single initial was a convention dating back to Mansfield Cumming-Smith, the first head of SIS (MI6), who became known as 'C' after his habit of initialling papers he had read with a C written in green ink. In Somerset Maugham's *Ashenden* stories, another source of inspiration for Fleming, the same post is occupied by 'R', the grim, amoral spy chief who is prepared to expend his agents ruthlessly without ever dirtying his own hands. Alongside the fictional R and the real C, there are three more Ms and one Z, all real, all known to Fleming, and all parts of the composite character that emerged as M.

'Colonel Z', Lieutenant Colonel Sir Claude Dansey, was Deputy Chief of SIS and head of the shadowy Z network of which Conrad O'Brien-Ffrench was a part. The bespectacled Dansey was witty, spiteful, charming and slightly mad. As a boy of sixteen, Dansey, who was not homosexual, was seduced by Oscar Wilde. His father threatened to prosecute, and then packed the young Claude off to Africa. He was first recruited as a spy during the Boer War, lost his money in the Wall Street Crash, performed various duties for British intelligence before the Second World War, and then abruptly quit, allowing rumours to circulate that he had been sacked for stealing. Meanwhile, believing SIS to be ill-organised and inefficient, he set about building a parallel organisation behind the cover of a respectable import–export business in Bush House, recruiting part-time, usually unpaid agents, including journalists, businessmen, gamblers and playboys. Dansey's agents used the codename Z, and avoided using the wireless for messages. In 1939, the Z network was absorbed into SIS, and as assistant to the new 'C', Stewart Menzies, Dansey helped to coordinate active espionage until the end of the war. Fleming gives him a namecheck in *From Russia with Love*, when Darko Kerim, Bond's friend who is murdered on the *Orient Express*, refers to 'Major Dansey', his predecessor as Head of Section T. Two famous men who worked in wartime intelligence with the real Dansey gave very different assessments of Colonel Z: Malcolm Muggeridge called him 'the only professional in MI6'; the historian Hugh Trevor-Roper, Lord Dacre, however, considered him 'an utter shit, corrupt, incompetent, but with a certain low cunning'.

Major-General Sir Colin McVean Gubbins was director of operations and training with SOE, and the creator of the auxiliary units on which Peter Fleming worked, intended to operate behind the lines in Britain in the event of a German invasion. An expert in guerrilla warfare, he was described by the cryptographer Leo Marks as 'a real Highland toughie, bloody brilliant . . . with a moustache which was as clipped as his delivery and eyes which didn't mirror his soul or any other such trivia. The general's eyes reflected the crossed swords on his shoulders, warning all comers not to cross them with him.' Since the initial C was already taken, and G is an initial commonly used as an army abbreviation, Gubbins signed himself by his middle initial: M.

Another contender is the equally strange MI5 spymaster Maxwell Knight, who ran a subsection of the security service responsible for rooting out potential extremist subversives in Britain, both fascist and communist. Knight broke up some of the most important spy rings in Britain, and was one of the first to warn that the secret services were being infiltrated by communist moles, but his warnings were fatally ignored. Knight was a man of many parts, most of them very odd and quite incompatible: in addition to running a huge and elaborate spy ring, he was a novelist, a jazz saxophonist who had been taught by the great Sidney Bechet, and an occultist who befriended and recruited the bizarre black magician Aleister Crowley. He was also an obsessive and inspired naturalist who kept snakes in the bath and wrote such definitive works as *How to Keep a Gorilla*. Ostensibly, Knight was a ladies' man: he was married three times (and briefly suspected of murdering one of his wives), filled his office with beautiful young women, ran two of the most successful female agents in British wartime history, and wrote a peculiar guide to running women agents, which includes a section on using sex as bait, in so-called honey traps. 'It is difficult to imagine anything more terrifying than for an officer to become landed with a woman-agent who suffers from an overdose of Sex,' he wrote. This slightly odd statement may perhaps be explained by the fact that Knight never consummated any of his marriages, and was probably homosexual. Maxwell Knight signed all his memos 'M', and was certainly well known to Fleming, although they never worked together. After the war, Knight would move effortlessly from a career in spying to a new career as a naturalist, ending his life as a much-loved BBC presenter of nature programmes.

There is one last real-life 'M', who may have helped to form the fictional M. William Melville, an Irish-born policeman who died in the last year of the First World War, has a good claim to be Britain's first secret service chief. Born in Kerry, Melville made his name foiling Fenian and anarchist bomb plots in Britain, and inspired the character of the detective in Joseph Conrad's *The Secret Agent*. Melville recruited Sidney Reilly, the so-called 'Ace of Spies', learned the art of lock-picking from Harry Houdini, and foiled the 1887 Golden Jubilee Plot to assassinate Queen Victoria. On his 'retirement' from the police in 1903, Melville founded a secret service, the forerunner of MI5, and adopted the codename 'M'. Using the pseudonym William Morgan, he gathered intelligence for the War Office, and when the Secret Service Bureau was established in 1909 to coordinate both home and foreign intelligence (later MI5 and MI6), Melville was recruited as chief detective. Fleming would certainly have been aware of the exploits of this other 'M', which had become a part of intelligence legend by the time he arrived at NID.

There is one final intriguing hypothesis, advanced by John Pearson, Fleming's biographer, to the effect that M might conceivably be modelled on Eve Fleming. Certainly, 'M' was Ian's nickname for his mother from early childhood. She, like M, was by turns strict and indulgent, loved and feared. As Pearson writes, 'While Fleming was young, his mother was certainly one of the few people he was frightened of, and her sternness toward him, her unexplained demands, and her remorseless insistence on success find a curious and constant echo in the way M handles that hard-ridden, hard-killing agent, 007.'

Who was Miss Moneypenny?

M's comely, love-struck secretary, the loyal keeper of secrets, has almost as many potential real lives as she has had appearances on screen. Miss Moneypenny's role in the books is comparatively small and, apart from her being a non-smoking, milk-drinking poodle-owner, we know little of her life. She 'would have been desirable but for eyes which were cool and direct and quizzical'. In *Thunderball* we learn that she 'often dreamed hopelessly about Bond'. Miss Moneypenny's yearning is made much more explicit in the films, and became a staple of the genre, the longest flirtation in film history, a central element in the badinage that precedes every Bond mission. Her amorous life is unfulfilled, but her career prospers, at least in the popular culture, as 'Britain's last line of defence'. By the time *You Only Live Twice* was filmed, she had been promoted to the rank of second officer in the Wrens, the Women's Royal Naval Service.

In the books Bond has his own secretary, Loelia Ponsonby, shared with 008 and 0011. The real Loelia Ponsonby was a friend of the Flemings who would become the Duchess of Westminster. When her marriage broke down, 'Lil' Ponsonby is said to have fallen for Ian himself, describing him as 'the most attractive man I've ever met'. For his part, Fleming described the fictional Loelia Ponsonby as 'tall and dark, with a reserved unbroken beauty', but added, 'unless she married soon, Bond thought for the hundredth time, or had a lover, her cool air of authority might easily become spinsterish' – which probably did not please the real 'Lil' one bit. It is possible that the duchess objected to seeing her real name hijacked for the purposes of popular literature. This may explain why, in *On Her Majesty's Secret Service*, Ponsonby abruptly retires after marrying a member of the Baltic Exchange ship-broking company, and is replaced as Bond's secretary by Mary Goodnight – a name with echoes of Fleming's own secretary at the *Sunday Times*, Una Trueblood (a name he would appropriate for the secretary murdered in *Dr No*). Both of Bond's secretaries are slight characters compared to Moneypenny, whose film persona is now almost as famous as Bond himself.

The name Moneypenny is derived from a character in an unfinished novel written by Peter Fleming after the war, entitled *The Sett*. The novel came to a halt after about thirty thousand words, but Miss Moneypenny survived in Ian's memory. The principal model for the Moneypenny character appears to have been a Miss Kathleen Pettigrew, who was the personal assistant to Stewart Menzies, Director General of MI6. In the first draft of *Casino Royale*, M's secretary was 'Miss Pettavel', or 'Petty', but Fleming clearly felt that was too close to reality and changed it. Miss Pettigrew was something of a legend in espionage circles: anyone attempting to gain access to 'C', as Fleming must have done, had first to pass through his terrifying secretary, who was brisk, intensely efficient and not remotely seductive. One former colleague described her as a 'formidable, grey-haired lady with the square jaw of the battleship type'.

Another strong possibility is Victoire 'Paddy' Bennett, who worked as a secretary in Room 39 and knew Fleming well. Bennett worked on 'Operation Mincemeat', the successful deception plan which involved planting a corpse with fake papers on the coast of Spain to persuade the Nazis that the Allies would attack Greece and Sardinia rather than Sicily. Ewen Montagu of NID was an architect of this ruse, and Fleming would probably have been at least tangentially involved. Paddy Bennett once described her former colleague, somewhat tartly, as 'definitely James Bond, in his mind'. She went on to marry Sir Julian Ridsdale, the long-serving MP for Harwich, and was made a Dame of the British Empire for her work with the Parliamentary Wives Club – a role that has a distinctly Moneypennyish ring to it.

Vera Atkins, executive officer with 'F' (French) Section, SOE, was described in her *New York Times* obituary in 2000 as 'widely believed to have inspired the character of Miss Moneypenny'. The unmarried Atkins was discreet, handsome and probably known to Fleming through his liaison duties. Though recruited as a secretary, Atkins swiftly emerged as a remarkable intelligence officer in her own right, briefing and dispatching more than five hundred SOE agents to occupied France; after the war she spent years trying to ascertain their fates.

In the end, Moneypenny was surely more fantasy than reality, not least because of the way Bond speaks to her. In *Thunderball*, when Moneypenny teases him about having to go to a health farm, he warns her: 'Any more ticking off from you and when I get out of this place I'll give you such a spanking you'll have to do your typing off a block of Dunlopillo.' Miss Moneypenny has an instant comeback: 'I don't think you'll be able to do much spanking after living on nuts and lemon juice for two weeks, James.' It is hard to imagine Fleming having such a conversation with any of the no-nonsense women he knew from wartime intelligence, let alone carrying out his spanking threat.

Villains, allies and others

'It is so difficult to make these villains frightening,' Fleming observed. 'But one is ashamed to overwrite them though that is probably what the public would like.' No one ever accused Fleming of *under*writing his villains, who are as lurid and sensational as Bond himself is deliberately understated. They are all extraordinary – ugly, deformed, brilliant, sadistic, rich, power-mad and unrepentantly insane. 'So was Frederick the Great,' crows Ernst Stavro Blofeld. 'So was Nietzsche, so was Van Gogh. We are in good, illustrious company . . .' Many have specific physical characteristics that mark them out as evil, or psychologically damaged, and usually both: an absence of earlobes, a gap between the front teeth, even red hair. Most are foreign, and a large proportion are German or Russian. Many are overweight, some astonishingly so – Blofeld tips the scales at thirty stone; several are wildly camp (Le Chiffre in *Casino Royale* addresses Bond as 'dear boy', Noël Coward's favourite form of address); Rosa Klebb is a lesbian; several villains are homosexual; and one is apparently an extreme opera fan – we meet Blofeld in *You Only Live Twice* dressed as a Valkyrie, complete with chainmail. These were not qualities, to put it mildly, that Fleming admired. Although some of Fleming's close friends were homosexual, he shared the prejudices of his time and class, and so does Bond. Fleming's villains do nothing by halves. Blofeld's criminal enterprises are 'on a scale of a Caligula, of a Nero, of a Hitler, of any of the greatest enemies of mankind'. Fleming's villains emerged out of a postwar world that had just witnessed, and defeated, wickedness on an unimaginable scale; yet some of the perpetrators of that evil – Mengele, Bormann and others – were still believed to be at large, and assumed to be living a life of criminal luxury. The criminal inventiveness of Bond's enemies seemed horribly believable in a world that had experienced the death camps, Japanese torture and Gestapo interrogation methods. Bond refers to friends who have been tortured during the war, and Fleming's personal knowledge of what could happen to captured agents again underpins the fiction. 'You only have to read about the many tortures used in the war by the Germans which were practised on several of our agents to realise that mine is mild stuff compared with that,' he once said.

Most of Bond's enemies are older, male, super-rich and sophisticated, a pattern that has prompted some to see Fleming's villains as caricatures of patriarchal figures. And it is certainly true that Bond is repeatedly brought to the villain's lair, told he is a young fool, and then prepared for punishment. This was a scene only too familiar to Fleming from many unpleasant encounters with his cane-wielding housemaster at Eton, and to any number of ex-public-schoolboys familiar with corporal punishment. 'My dear boy,' Le Chiffre spoke, like a father, 'the game of Red Indians is over, quite over. You have stumbled by mischance into a game for grown-ups.' Bond's ability to trip up the patronising crooks and bullies had an instant appeal to every grown-up schoolboy who still dreamed of kicking the headmaster in the groin.

Once more, Fleming's villains, like his heroes, are patch-works of different people, names and traits. Le Chiffre, the sweaty, Benzedrine-sniffing villain of *Casino Royale*, is believed to be based on Aleister Crowley, who gained huge notoriety in inter-war Britain as 'The Wickedest Man in the World'. Crowley was a bisexual, sado-masochistic drug addict with the ears of a leprechaun and the eyes of a dissipated stoat. A master of Thelemic mysticism ('Do what thou wilt shall be the whole of the Law'), he specialised in mountaineering, interpreting the Ouija board, orgies and thrashing his lovers. The press simultaneously adored and hated him. Crowley made Le Chiffre seem positively sane.

Oddly enough, Crowley is also claimed to have been a British spy. The *International Journal of Intelligence and Counter-intelligence* recorded that, while living in America during the First World War, Crowley used the cover of a German propagandist to gather information for the British secret service on the German intelligence network in the United States, and on Irish Republican activity. During the Second World War, Crowley personally offered to make contact with Rudolf Hess, Hitler's deputy, who was thought to be fascinated by the occult. After Hess landed in Scotland,

Crowley offered to intercede as a sort of mystical go-between: 'If it is true that Herr Hess is much influenced by Astrology and magick, my services might be of use,' he wrote. Fleming was clearly intrigued, and suggested using Crowley to supply Hess with fake horoscopes, or as an interrogator. After all, Crowley and Hess spoke the same language, namely gobbledegook. Neither idea came to fruition, but Crowley had plainly made a strong impression.

Fleming plundered his school register ruthlessly in the quest for names. Hugo Drax, the villain in *Moonraker*, was named after the magnificently festooned Admiral Sir Reginald Aylmer Ranfurly Plunkett-Ernle-Erle-Drax, an acquaintance of Fleming's who led the pre-war military mission to Moscow in 1939 to discuss a possible alliance with the USSR. Ernst Stavro Blofeld, the super-villain without earlobes (he also has no cats in the novels; that had to wait for the movies), was probably named after another Old Etonian, Tom Blofeld, a farmer from Norfolk whose son Henry Blofeld is the much-loved, plummy-voiced BBC cricket commentator. Alternatively, Blofeld may owe his name to China scholar John Blofeld, who was a member of Fleming's club, Boodles, and whose father was named Ernst. Red Grant, the assassin in *From Russia with Love*, was the name of a cheerful river guide Fleming knew in Jamaica, and Francisco 'Pistols' Scaramanga, the triple-nippled gunman in *The Man with the Golden Gun*, was named after yet another school contemporary, George Scaramanga. Fleming and Scaramanga are said to have had a number of schoolyard fights. Fleming got his revenge in print. (The original Scaramanga had the regulation number of nipples.)

While most of Fleming's friends and acquaintances enjoyed appearing in the series, a few objected vehemently. In *Diamonds Are Forever,* Fleming described the homosexual villain 'Boofy' Kidd: 'Kidd's a pretty boy. His friends call him "Boofy" . . . some of these homos make the worst killers.' This was all very well, but one of Fleming's best friends (and a relative of his wife, Ann) was Arthur Gore, later the Earl of Arran, who was universally known by the distinctive nickname 'Boofy'. Gore was livid and complained bitterly, to no avail.

Another who strongly objected to seeing his name in a Bond novel was Ernö Goldfinger, the distinguished and controversial modernist architect. Fleming first heard the name from his golfing partner, John Blackwell, who was a cousin by marriage of Ernö Goldfinger and disliked him. Fleming is said to have objected to Goldfinger's love of concrete and the destruction of Victorian houses to make way for his tower blocks. According to one theory, Fleming particularly hated a terrace of modern houses designed by Goldfinger on Willow Road in Hampstead, and so used his name for one of his most memorable evildoers: Auric Goldfinger, the richest man in England; treasurer of the Soviet counter-intelligence agency, SMERSH; and a gold-obsessive who likes to paint his lovers with gold in order to make love to the substance he craves. When Ernö obtained a proof copy of *Goldfinger*, he gave it to his associate, Jacob Blacker, and asked him whether he should sue. Blacker read the book and reported that the only substantial difference was: 'You're called Ernö and he's called Auric.' This was rather rude, since Ernö was a visionary six-foot architect and Auric is a murderous five-foot megalomaniac. But, unlike most of Fleming's name-borrowings, there are a few genuine similarities between the Goldfingers: both were Jewish émigrés from Eastern Europe who liked fast cars, and both were Marxists, in Auric's case by association with SMERSH. There is also a whiff of anti-Semitism in Fleming's depiction of a Jewish billionaire with a gold fixation. The real Goldfinger was exceptionally unamused, summoned his lawyers, and threatened to halt publication. Equally angry, Fleming thought his publisher should insert an erratum slip, changing Goldfinger to 'Goldprick' throughout the book (a name originally suggested, unseriously, by the critic Cyril Connolly). A truce was established after Fleming's publishers agreed that, in advertising the book, the name Goldfinger would be coupled with the name Auric wherever possible. Even so, for the rest of his life Ernö Goldfinger was plagued by people calling him on the telephone and saying, in the voice of Sean Connery, 'Goldfinger? This is 007.'

Ernö provided the name, unwittingly and unwillingly, but the character of Goldfinger may have been based on the extrovert and flashy American gold tycoon Charles W. Engelhard Jr, whom Fleming met in 1949 and remained friends with. Engelhard was owner of a huge mining and metals conglomerate, and a major racehorse owner. The gold magnate delighted in the general assumption that he was the inspiration for Goldfinger, turning up to parties dressed in orange and pretending that he had a stewardess named Pussy Galore on his private plane.

'Q', the head of research and development for the secret service and irascible provider of Bond's gadgets and cars, would become a staple character in the films, but there is no Q character in the books. In *Casino Royale*, Bond is told to 'see Q for any equipment you need', but this is most likely to be a reference to 'Q-Branch', the real name of a shadowy department which supplied uniforms, gizmos and other unconventional weapons of war. Charles Fraser-Smith of Q-Branch had provided much of the equipment for Operation Ruthless, Fleming's aborted plan to capture the Enigma codebook. A former missionary in Morocco, Fraser-Smith was nominally a civil servant with the Ministry of Supply's Clothing and Textile Department, under cover of which he made equipment for secret agents, saboteurs and prisoners of war, such as miniature cameras, maps written in invisible ink and golf balls hollowed out to hide a compass. When this latter technique was used to conceal diamonds in the film of *Diamonds Are Forever*, Fraser-Smith was critical, pointing out that the golf balls he had designed during the war were ideal secret receptacles since they would still work as golf balls, whereas those imagined in the film would barely have got off the ground.

Fleming clearly derived great pleasure, and considerable devilry, from his choice of names, whether the subject was good, bad or inanimate. He had an extraordinary ear for names with a ring to them, a gift which later imitators have found hard to emulate. 'He took immense trouble with names and plots, although the names sometimes came before the plots,' said his friend Ivar Bryce (whose own name would be adopted by Bond as an alias in *Live and Let Die*). 'He enjoyed using the names of his friends, or even those he only knew slightly.' Or not at all. People were named after things, and things were named after people. His lover in later life, Blanche Blackwell, gave him a small boat named *Octopussy*, which became the name of a man-eating pet octopus in the short story. In rather ungallant return, Fleming named the ancient guano tanker in *Dr No* the *Blanche*. The crime boss Marc-Ange Draco in *On Her Majesty's Secret Service* is named after El Draco, the Spanish name for the English privateer Sir Francis Drake – a reference picked up years later by J. K. Rowling for her Hogwarts antihero, Draco Malfoy. Rosa Klebb (the Russian for bread) was partly based on Colonel Rybkin of Soviet intelligence. Major Boothroyd, the secret service armourer, is named in honour of Geoffrey Boothroyd, the gun expert who provided

Fleming with invaluable technical advice. Ernie Cuneo, a hard-nosed New York lawyer and friend of Fleming, found himself turned into Ernie Cureo, the Las Vegas taxi-driver and undercover CIA agent in *Diamonds Are Forever*; his American friends Tommy and Oatsie Leiter became Felix Leiter, Bond's CIA ally. One of the more charming christenings was that of Vesper Lynd in *Casino Royale*. One afternoon in Jamaica, Fleming and Ivar Bryce visited a romantically isolated mansion on the coast and were ushered in to meet 'The Colonel'. A little later, a dusty butler appeared and announced, 'Vespers are served', while dishing up a powerful concoction of rum, herbs, fruit and ice. Ever after, Fleming associated the word Vesper with a heady sort of glamour, and made her Bond's first lover. Darko Kerim, the extrovert secret service agent in *From Russia with Love*, was based on Nazim Kalkavan, Fleming's guide to Istanbul when he covered an Interpol conference there in 1956.

Fleming teased his friends and acquaintances by putting them, their names, or their characteristics in his books. But the character he most pillaged for material was himself. It is a measure of Fleming's introspection that he could identify his own virtues as well as his vices, and inject them both into the personality of James Bond. In Bond's obituary in *The Times*, from *You Only Live Twice*, Fleming cannot resist the opportunity to write his own epitaph, with a knowing glimmer of self-congratulation:

To serve the confidential nature of his work, he was accorded the rank of lieutenant in the Special Branch of the RNVR, and it is a measure of the satisfaction his services gave to his superiors that he ended the war with the rank of commander.

THE PLOTS: FROM HOT WAR TO COLD WAR

The Plots:
From Hot War to Cold War

James Bond is a warrior of the Cold War. Yet in many ways – in attitude, sensibility and even equipment – he is a creation of the Second World War. As with Fleming himself, that war shaped and toughened him, and with the ending of that conflict, in common with many combatants, he finds himself adrift. In *From Russia with Love*, Bond's war nostalgia is made explicit: 'He was a man of war and when, for a long period, there was no war, his spirit went into a decline.'

Ian Fleming shared with his brother, Peter, a fear that Britain, having triumphed over Nazism, was becoming soft and irrelevant, a land of small minds and smaller dreams. In this, they echoed the views of a generation brought up to think of Britain as Great, but now doomed in peacetime to watch the American ascendancy, decolonisation, queues, bureaucracy, socialism and other perceived indignities as the

Empire declined. In Fleming's words: 'The blubbery arms of the soft life had Bond round the neck and they were slowly strangling him . . . in his particular line of business, peace had reigned for nearly a year, and peace was killing him.' For many of the men and women who had fought Nazism for six long years, peace was an almost physical jolt. Amid the fear and deprivations of war, many had experienced excitement, danger and a freedom from the daily drudgery of normal life in ways that would never be repeated. Even men like Fleming, who had fought a relatively comfortable war of the intellect, had been stretched and challenged. Victory brought peace, but it also brought boredom: 'The only vice Bond utterly condemned.'

Fleming himself was easily bored. He was bored by shooting parties in Scotland, stockbroking, small talk and his wife's literary soirées. He was bored as only a member of the upper class who has never had to work hard can be bored. He was temperamentally inclined to boredom, and alarmed by its effect on his moods. The very first lines of *Casino Royale* are suffused with ennui: 'The soul-erosion produced by high gambling – a compost of fear and greed and nervous tension – becomes unbearable and the senses awake and revolt from it.' Fleming's villains suffer from the affliction as well as his hero. 'Mister Bond, I suffer from boredom,' declares Mr Big in *Live and Let Die*. 'I am a prey to what the early Christians called "accidie" – the deadly lethargy that envelops those who are sated . . .' Fleming spent much of his life trying to escape boredom, seeking new thrills, new locations, new cars, new lovers. 'There was only one way to deal with boredom – kick oneself out of it,' he wrote in *From Russia with Love*. Fleming's novels were a cure for boredom, his own and that of his readers: his inspiration was to take the reality and spirit of the Second World War – British self-belief, technological wizardry, and above all the sense of moral rectitude in an honourable cause – and apply it to the far more murky world of the Cold War.

In his novel *The Sixth Column*, published in 1951, Peter Fleming wrote of Britain's need for a buccaneering hero 'with the urbane, faintly swashbuckling sangfroid of Raffles', as an 'antidote to the restrictions and frustrations of life in England'. For Ian Fleming, the veteran of wartime intelligence, a patriotic spy at war, whether cold or hot, was simply 'the most exciting of all human adventure stories – the single man, in the darkness, facing death alone for the sake of the great mass of his countrymen'. Bond is a world-saver, just as Britain perceived itself to be during the war; American intelligence is secondary to that of Britain. Indeed, the Americans rely on Bond: when the evil forces of SMERSH seek to attack the West, their primary target is Bond, and Bond alone, who must be killed 'with ignominy'. Fleming played on contemporary fears to give Bond modern relevance, but his hero harks back to wartime figures like Patrick Dalzel-Job and Fitzroy Maclean, the ideal antidote to Britain's postwar austerity, rationing and the looming premonition of lost power.

As the two superpowers, the USA and USSR, fought it out in an escalating arms race, Britons could, through Bond and his exploits, relive a fast-disappearing world where Britain called the shots, and won the war. 'You underestimate the English,' Bond warns Goldfinger. 'They may be slow, but they get there.' This was, of course, fantasy – Britain's power was eroding fast, and in the great espionage confrontation between the CIA and the KGB, Britain's SIS was no more than a minor player. In the 1950s, the British intelligence establishment was rocked by the exposure of an entire Soviet spy network within its ranks: the defections of Guy Burgess and Donald Maclean represented a body blow to the prestige and self-confidence of the British secret service. So far from dominating the espionage battle against communism, British intelligence was viewed with mounting, and entirely justified, suspicion by the CIA. In 1965, Lyndon Johnson ordered a secret investigation into the entire structure of British intelligence. For most of the war, Britain had conducted the espionage battle against Germany with remarkable results; by 1952, the conductor's baton had passed to the US, and Britain was firmly in the position of second fiddle.

Ian Fleming simply ignored this inconvenient fact. His fantasy of an omnipotent British secret service nourished millions of readers on both sides of the Atlantic, and spread velyn Beatrice Ste Croix Fleming (née ose), Ian Fleming's beautiful, domineering 1other, who was known to the young leming boys, intriguingly, as 'M'.

Valentine Fleming, Fleming's adored father, who was killed in action while serving on the Western Front in 1917.

he four Fleming brothers: Ian, Michael, eter and Richard. 'Strong, handsome, lack-haired, blue-eyed boys', as one ontemporary described them.

Ian with his mother on the beach. In his writings, Fleming recalled his childhood beach holidays with a deep and nostalgic affection, which he transferred to James Bond.

Fleming (*second from right*) attending a dining club at Eton.
His younger brother Richard is seated to his right.

Fleming clad in his naval
uniform in Room 39 of the
Admiralty, the nerve centre
of the Naval Intelligence
Division. It was a smoky
den crammed with desks,
which one inhabitant likened
to 'an Arab bank'.

Stockbroker.	DESCRIPTION SIGNALEMENT	PHOTOGRAPH OF BEARER
~~PRESS (REUTERS)~~		

DESCRIPTION — SIGNALEMENT

Profession / Profession

Place and date of birth / Lieu et date de naissance ... 28 ... 1908

Domicile / Domicile ... Eng...

Height / Taille ... 6 ... ft ... in ... ft ... in

Colour of eyes / Couleur des yeux

Colour of hair / Couleur de cheveux

Special peculiarities / Signes particuliers

WIFE — FEMME

(photo)

CHILDREN — ENFANTS

Name / Nom	... of birth / ... de naissance	Sex / Sexe

...eming's passport, showing his career switch from journalism, at which he had excelled, to
...ockbroking, at which he was quite hopeless.

УДОСТОВЕРЕНИЕ

№ 21

Отдел печати Народного Комиссариата по Иностранным Делам удостоверяет, что гражданин Ян Ланкастер Флеминг действительно зарегистрирован как корреспондент „Таймс"

Срок настоящего удостоверения продлен
по 193 г.

Зав. Отд. печати НКИД

Срок настоящего удостоверения продлен
по 193 г.

Зав. Отд. печати НКИД

Срок настоящего удостоверения продлен
по 193 г.

Зав. Отд. печати НКИД

Действительно по 23/V 193 г.

Зав. Отд. печати НКИД

...e Soviet press pass issued to Fleming in 1939.

Norman Parkinson's portrait of Ian Fleming in suitably James Bond-like pose. Fleming disliked shooting and knew little about guns, avoiding them whenever possible.

Monique Panchaud de Bottomes, the Swiss woman to whom Fleming became briefly engaged in 1931 while studying French and German at the University of Geneva.

Muriel Wright, Fleming's wartime lover: a model, athlete and good-time girl, who was tragically killed during the bombing of London. Fleming mourned 'Mu' deeply after her death, and perhaps modelled the archetypal Bond Girl on her.

Ian with Ann Fleming, the woman he married in 1952. Their marriage was complex and often painful, but it was also loving and full of humour.

Patrick Dalzel-Job, the naval intelligence officer and commando whose extraordinary exploits during the Second World War brought him into contact with Ian Fleming. Dalzel-Job was one of the principal inspirations for the character of 007.

Wilfred 'Biffy' Dunderdale, the debonair station chief of MI6 in Paris, whose contacts with French and Polish intelligence helped to secure a model of the Enigma machine and break the German code.

Sir Fitzroy Maclean of Dunconnel: Scottish diplomat, soldier, adventurer, writer and politician, and another model for James Bond.

ernard Lee in the role of 'M', James Bond's ascible and indulgent boss. In *The Man ith the Golden Gun*, Fleming finally reveals s name: Vice Admiral Sir Miles Messervy, CMG.

Rear Admiral John Godfrey, Fleming's boss as Director of Naval Intelligence, and the principal model for 'M'. Grumpy and demanding, Godfrey was nonetheless 'a real war winner', in Fleming's estimation.

Maxwell Knight, the wartime MI5 agent-runner who signed his memoirs 'M', and who ended his life as a much-loved presenter of nature programmes on the BBC.

Vera Atkins, executive officer with the French section of the Special Operations Executive (SOE), and a brilliant intelligence professional who spent many years after the war seeking to discover the fate of her agents.

Lois Maxwell played the role of Miss Moneypenny, 'Britain's last line of defence' in the first fourteen James Bond films.

Ursula Andress on the beach in *Dr No*, wearing that bikini or, technically speaking, a black and white front-gather underwire bra with widely spaced shoulder straps and nombril bikini. And a knife.

a legend of British espionage efficiency that persists to this day. In a now-notorious speech of 2003, President George W. Bush implicitly summoned up the ghost of James Bond when he cited British intelligence as a reason for invading Iraq: 'The British government has learned that Saddam Hussein recently sought significant quantities of uranium from Africa.' French spy work, say, or even American intelligence, would not have carried quite the same cachet. The information about African uranium was wrong, but that is not the point here: Fleming and Bond spread the belief that Britain produced the best spies in the world and, bizarrely, the myth stuck.

Fleming's characters and plots emerge, in many instances, directly from the Second World War. Even the demonology derives from that conflict: evildoers being, in approximate order of untrustworthiness, German, Russian, Japanese, Bulgarian, Korean and French. Characters are endowed with realistic, and often elaborate, past histories, to place them more firmly in the present. Polish-born Blofeld, we discover, spied for Germany during the war. The brutal communist Le Chiffre was found wandering in the Dachau displaced persons camp, apparently suffering from amnesia. He has no name; he is merely the number, '*le chiffre*'. The ghastly Rosa Klebb, the colonel in charge of operations and executions for SMERSH, is given an earlier career in the Spanish Civil War, working for Andrés Nin, the Spanish communist revolutionary. Nin was tortured and murdered, on Stalin's orders, in 1937. Fleming implies that his murderer was the fictional Klebb.

Many of the names chosen by Fleming were German, an unsubtle code to indicate that the Nazi menace was still at large: Egon Bartsch and Dr Walter are German scientists who worked on the Nazi rocket programme employed by Drax on the Moonraker project; Bruno Bayer is a former Gestapo agent now working for SPECTRE. Drax himself is really former Nazi officer Graf Hugo von der Drache ('*Drache*' being German for dragon), and his aide de camp is Willy Krebs, a name at least some of Fleming's readers would have recognised – General Hans Krebs was Hitler's army chief of staff, who committed suicide in the Führer's bunker shortly after Hitler himself.

Bond's allies have seen war service: Leiter is a former captain with the US Marines; in *Moonraker*, 008 has returned from Peenemunde, site of the wartime rocket research facility in northern Germany; even Mary Goodnight, Bond's secretary, is an ex-Wren. Bond was born at a time when memoirs and biographies of Second World War personalities were being published in large numbers, revealing a real world of derring-do that came as a revelation to many readers. That individuals had carried out acts of unbelievable bravery in the war made Bond that much more believable. The Second World War provides the psychological backdrop for almost all the principal characters. 'He was back there again fighting war,' Fleming writes of Tiger Tanaka, the spy trained as a kamikaze pilot who heads the Japanese secret service in *You Only Live Twice*. 'Bond knew the symptoms. He often visited this haunted forest of memory himself.' Or as Bond remarks in *Thunderball*: 'The war just doesn't seem to have ended for us.'

The clues to the Second World War are everywhere, yet Bond is fighting an emphatically new war, against a looming communist threat, in the shape of its most evil and ruthless manifestation, SMERSH. Once again, Fleming drew on reality and reshaped it to lend credibility to this imagined combat. The people, the weapons, the scenes, all carried deliberate echoes of real wartime events. The underwater trap door in the hull of the *Disco Volante* in *Thunderball* and the limpet-mining of Mr Big's boat in *Live and Let Die* may well be based on the extraordinary wartime activities of the 10th Light Flotilla, an elite unit of Italian navy frogmen, who used similar methods to attack Allied shipping off Gibraltar in what Fleming considered 'the greatest piece of effrontery in the underwater war'. The assassination attempt on Bond in *Casino Royale* was, according to Fleming himself, based on the attempted Soviet assassination in 1942 of the former spymaster Franz von Papen, then Germany's ambassador to Turkey: in both fact and fiction, the assassins were Bulgarians acting as Soviet agents, and in both cases they failed to kill the target and blew themselves up instead.

If some of Fleming's plots transposed Second World War

events into a Cold War setting, others were drawn directly from the events of the Cold War itself. Real people, such as Lavrenty Beria, chief of Soviet security and one of Stalin's principal executioners, are mentioned to lend authenticity: the fall of Beria (executed on the orders of Khrushchev in 1953) enables Grubozaboyschikov to become head of SMERSH and allows Rosa Klebb to take over Otydel II, in charge of operation and execution. Interestingly, Fleming states that Beria 'went to the gallows' on 13 January 1954, the official Soviet date of the execution; after the files were later opened, however, it was revealed that Beria had been shot almost a month earlier. Such mingling of fact and fiction is deliberate and highly effective. Fleming occupied a world radically divided between the communist East and the capitalist West, and one that was intensely paranoid. The *Thunderball* plot imagined Blofeld threatening to bomb Miami with stolen atomic weapons, eerily foreshadowing the 1962 Cuban Missile Crisis. To contemporary readers, that menace seemed only too real. Indeed, the failure of the Bay of Pigs invasion and the Cuban crisis reinforced fear of the Soviet threat, and boosted the sales of Fleming's books.

Indeed, for a time Bond was physically as close to the action of the Cold War as it was possible to get: namely, on the bedside table of the President of the United States. John F. Kennedy was first introduced to Fleming's books in 1955, and read a copy of *Casino Royale* while convalescing in New England. He remained a fan to the end of his life. In 1961, Kennedy named *From Russia with Love* in his top ten favourite books, an endorsement that did no harm to his image, and did wonders for Fleming's US sales. A subsequent advertisement featured a picture of the White House with a single window lit and the caption: 'You can bet on it he's reading one of those Ian Fleming thrillers.' The enthusiasm was not limited to JFK: Robert Kennedy was also a keen reader, and their sister Eunice read every novel at least once. 'The entire Kennedy family is crazy about James Bond,' Fleming was told. The President insisted on showing the film of *Dr No* at a private screening in the White House. Fleming returned the compliment: one of the few books Bond has in his library is Kennedy's *Profiles in Courage*. The Kennedys gave Bond an immense boost, but then 007 was useful, in turn, to the Kennedys: it did the President's reputation no harm whatever to be thought to be sitting up at night, reading novels about a tough, handsome anti-communist who was irresistible to women.

Fleming met JFK just once, in 1960, before he was elected to the presidency, when the English writer was invited to a dinner party at Kennedy's home in Washington DC. The conversation inevitably turned to Castro and Cuba. Fleming – with tongue, one suspects, firmly in cheek – suggested that leaflets be scattered over Cuba warning that radioactivity could lodge in beards and that they should all therefore shave, thus potentially ridiculing the famously over-bearded

Castro. This sounds merely silly, and it was, but no sillier than the various lunatic efforts to dislodge the Cuban strong man that were being actively discussed within the CIA. Bizarrely, one of the other dinner party guests, a CIA agent, passed Fleming's idea on to his boss. Once again, Fleming's imagination merged with fantastic reality. The crucial, mutually advantageous relationship between Bond and Kennedy is illustrated by one final, perhaps apocryphal, detail. The night before he was assassinated in Dallas, the President is said to have been reading a James Bond novel; so was Lee Harvey Oswald, the man who would kill him the very next day.

If Fleming's Cold War plots seemed outlandish at times, he was unapologetic. This was an age in which presidents read novels and novelists advised presidents, and it did not, for instance, seem impossible to the CIA that it could kill Fidel Castro by injecting his cigars with poison. The spy war was, at times, truly bizarre, and the more weird it was, the more Fleming was impelled to echo it in fiction. The attempt by SMERSH to assassinate Bond on the *Orient Express* in *From Russia with Love* was based directly on the death of Eugene Karp. A US naval attaché (and spy) in Romania, Karp was apparently on the run from Soviet assassins when he boarded the famous train in Bucharest in February 1950. His body was found later by ramblers in a railway tunnel near Salzburg. The train conductor had apparently been drugged, but officials claimed Karp had fallen out of a door; everyone else, including Fleming, believed he had been killed by Soviet assassins, a murder on the *Orient Express*. If that sounded like pure fantasy (Agatha Christie had published *Murder on the Orient Express* in 1934), Fleming was quick to point out that Cold War reality, and the espionage game, was stranger than any fiction he could invent:

> My plots are fantastic, while often being based on truth. They go wildly beyond the probable, but not, I think, beyond the possible. Every now and then there will be a story in the newspapers that lifts a corner of the veil from Secret Service work. A tunnel from East to West Berlin so that our Secret Service can tap the Russian telephone system; Crabb's frogman exploit to examine the hull of a Soviet cruiser; the Russian spy Khokhlov with his cigarette case that fired dum-dum bullets . . . this is all true Secret Service history that is yet in the higher realm of fantasy, and James Bond's ventures into this realm are perfectly legitimate.

These real events cited by Fleming are worth exploring in greater detail, since they reflect the remarkable dovetailing of truth and fiction in the Bond stories. The name of Commander Lionel 'Buster' Crabb will for ever be linked with the more outlandish antics of the British secret service.

In 1956, this Royal Navy frogman was recruited by MI6 to inspect the hull of the Soviet cruiser that had brought Nikita Khrushchev on a state visit to Britain. Crabb's mission was probably to search for mine-laying hatches and sonar equipment on the bottom of the Soviet ship as it lay in Portsmouth harbour. The MI6 officer in charge of the mission was Nicholas Elliott, a friend of Fleming's. Crabb was unfit; the mission was idiotic, diplomatically unwise and exceedingly dangerous. It was, needless to say, a disaster. Crabb's headless body was found off the coast fourteen months later. The Crabb affair prompted outrage, a diplomatic firestorm, the resignation of MI6 director John Sinclair, and a flood of speculation that continues unabated. But it proved to the public that the British secret service was still capable of the most extravagant adventures. Three years later, Fleming sent Bond out to investigate the hull of the *Disco Volante* in *Thunderball*; unlike Crabb, he returns intact, just.

If Crabb was the Western spy who failed, then Nikolai Khokhlov was the Soviet spy who very nearly succeeded. A KGB spy whose exploits rival any of the models on which Bond was based, Khokhlov had fought behind the lines in the Second World War, and had taken part in the assassination of the Nazi official Wilhelm Kube, then Generalkommissar for White Russia. Khokhlov's spymaster was Pavel Sudoplatov, head of the Administration for Special Tasks in the NKVD (which would become the KGB), in charge of sabotage and assassinations. From the seventh floor of the dreaded Lubyanka building, Sudoplatov plotted the deaths of those perceived as enemies of the regime, including the murder of Trotsky in 1940. In 1953, Khokhlov was selected by Sudoplatov to assassinate a prominent anti-Soviet Russian émigré in Berlin. Khokhlov, a man of conscience, found he could not carry out such a murder in cold blood, and instead defected to the West, bringing with him an extraordinary array of murderous gadgetry, including two guns housed in metal cigarette cases, which could fire up to four hollow steel bullets, and a miniature revolver that fired poisoned bullets. Khokhlov's defection was a sensation, but perhaps still more astounding was the Soviet riposte: in 1957, while attending a conference in Frankfurt, Khokhlov drank a cup of coffee that had been laced with radioactive thallium. Its effects were terrifying. Khokhlov's face erupted in black, brown and blue lumps, his eyes oozed a sticky liquid and his hair fell out in handfuls. The blood in his veins began to turn to plasma, as his bones crumbled. Astonishingly, Khokhlov survived, thanks to repeated transfusions by American doctors working around the clock. Khokhlov was still alive when this book was being written, living in quiet retirement in San Bernardino, California, an astonishing monument to Soviet ruthlessness and his own resilience. Khokhlov's remarkable book, *In the Name of Conscience*, was published in 1959. A copy inevitably found its way on to Fleming's bookshelves, and from there into his fiction. The gun concealed inside a copy of *War and Peace* and wielded by the Soviet assassin Red Grant in *From Russia with Love* owed its inception to the Khokhlov haul of assassination gadgetry. In an interview in 2006, Khokhlov told me: 'The KGB decided to kill me . . . From this moment there was a general direction to hunt Khokhlov. The message was: "We will get the traitor, wherever he is in the world."' This, of course, was precisely the role of SMERSH, both in Fleming's books, and in reality.

Thanks to James Bond, SMERSH became a household name, but few realise that such an organisation really existed, long before Fleming gave it wicked immortality. In the bewildering forest of acronyms that was the Soviet secret service, SMERSH was just one of many names by which the specialised counter-intelligence department of the Soviet Union was known. SMERSH, as Fleming writes, is formed by combining the Russian words '*Smyert*' and '*Shpionam*', meaning (approximately) 'death to spies'. Within Soviet intelligence, this unit (which would eventually report directly to Stalin) was responsible for rooting out and killing spies, saboteurs and 'criminal traitors'. Fleming had learned about SMERSH from Colonel Grigori Tokaty-Tokaev, a Soviet rocket specialist who defected to Britain in 1947. In fact, a year earlier, the real SMERSH had been absorbed into the People's Commissariat of Military Forces, but Fleming decided to retain the chilling name. In this, his fiction may inadvertently have been shadowing the truth, for it is believed that certain elements within the original SMERSH continued to operate throughout the 1950s as assassination squads. In *Live and Let Die*, 'Bond felt his spine crawl at the cold, brilliant efficiency of the Soviet machine, and at the fear of death and torture which made it work.'

This, then, is Bond's political world: a world of ruthless Soviet killers, in which the pride of the British secret service hold back the horrors of communism and defend freedom almost single-handedly. True, Bond is prey to the odd flicker of doubt, and the occasional rueful political reflection, at least initially. In *Casino Royale*, he allows himself to wonder about the shifting sands of politics: 'This country right-or-wrong business is getting a little out of date. Today we are fighting Communism . . . History is moving pretty quickly these days, and the heroes and villains keep changing parts.' The reference to the fallout from the Burgess and Maclean scandal is clear. Felix Leiter, Bond's CIA ally, nonetheless 'held the interests of his own organisation far above the mutual concerns of the North Atlantic Allies'. What is more, 'Bond sympathised with him', as well he might. Does Bond, in his heart, know that the British secret service is not quite all it is cracked up to be? M warns him, in an unguarded moment, that Tiger Tanaka, the head of the Japanese secret service, may have little respect for British intelligence: 'People don't these days,' the spymaster reflects glumly. In *You Only Live Twice*, Tanaka voices Fleming's own fears about a once-great country falling into post-colonial lethargy: a 'vacuous, aimless, horde of seekers-after-pleasure'. Fleming feared that Britain had become a browbeaten nation of obedient people standing in line, the state of British malaise Churchill himself referred to as 'Queuetopia'. Bond's defence is not terribly convincing: 'Balls to you, Tiger. You only judge people by your own jungle standards . . . the liberation of our colonies may have gone too fast, but we still climb Everest and beat plenty of the world at plenty of sports and win plenty of Nobel Prizes . . .'

By the 1960s, the myth of Britain taking on the Soviet menace was becoming impossible to sustain. As Fleming wrote in his 1960 short story 'The Hildebrand Rarity', 'There were really only three powers. That was the big poker game and no other country had either the chips or the cards to come into it.' The sentiment is expressed by the American villain Milton Krest, but it was a reality Fleming and Bond now had to accept. In another short story, 'Quantum of Solace', the British Empire is described as 'crumbling', and the plot of *You Only Live Twice* centres on Bond's attempt to obtain secret information, to which the Americans will no longer allow Britain access, from the Japanese. 'At home and abroad,' Bond confides to Kerim in *From Russia with Love*, 'we don't show teeth any more – only gums.'

From 1960 onwards, Bond's enemies are no longer the Soviet menace, but individual crooks and killers, gangsters of the higher variety, and most notably SPECTRE (the Special Executive for Counter-Intelligence, Terrorism, Revenge and Extortion), the crime syndicate staffed by ex-members of SMERSH, the Gestapo, the Mafia and the Black Tong of Peking, and run by Blofeld. The shift of focus is even more emphatic in the films. Where once Bond battled ideological foes, in his latter-day incarnations he takes on freelance bandits, mafia types and criminal megalomaniacs – terrifying but politically neutral. The Americans still need bailing out, but no longer is there any pretence of British supremacy. The enemies of the later novels brilliantly antic-ipate modern threats: Colombian drugs cartels and Russian mafia bosses, as well as the lone maverick megalomaniacs, Osama bin Ladens *avant la lettre*. Bond's evolution from Cold War warrior to international crime-fighter reflects the changing preoccupations of the times, but also Fleming's need to ensure that beneath the fantasy lay a realistic foun-dation: here were new battles, with new enemies that Bond and Britain could realistically fight and, more importantly, defeat.

Unlike his film incarnation, Bond is not immune to doubt, but the moments when he is on the back foot are rare indeed: his is a universe where Britain triumphs, America follows, the British secret service is supreme, communists and criminals are defeated, and the globe is a better place for it. One may dismiss all of this as propagandist fantasy (many did just that, particularly on the other side of the

Iron Curtain), but the world Fleming described was, in some deeper sense than mere reality, true. In the real world, secret agents did not go around sticking limpet mines on ships, torturing their enemies, or killing one another with poisoned bullets fired from cigarette cases. Except that they did, and they still do. As you read this, secret agents are working undercover to track down individuals mad enough to threaten the world by stealing atomic missiles or threatening biological warfare, in the manner of Blofeld. The fear of weapons of mass destruction permeates our world, just as it runs through the Bond books. And in London, an outspoken Russian defector dies after agents unknown slip radioactive poison into his food.

How much of James Bond is true? Fleming himself joked that 'if the quality of these books, or their degree of veracity, had been any higher, the author would have certainly been prosecuted under the Official Secrets Act'. Perhaps the most pleasing irony is that, even today, MI6 itself is a little ambivalent about where James Bond ends and real life begins. The official MI6 website (www.sis.gov.uk) asks, 'How realistic is the depiction of SIS in the James Bond films?' but then only half-answers the question. 'James Bond, as Ian Fleming originally conceived him, was based on reality . . . But any author needs to inject a level of glamour and excitement beyond reality in order to sell.' Yet the spy agency cannot bring itself to deny its greatest asset. 'Nevertheless,' continues the article, 'staff who join

SIS can look forward to a career that will have moments when the gap narrows just a little and the certainty of a stimulating and rewarding career which, like Bond's, will be in the service of their country.'

James Bond is now an MI6 recruiter. A real spy agency, harnessing fiction, based on fact, to recruit real spies: no one would have been more flattered than Ian Fleming.

005

GADGETS, GUNS, GIZMOS AND GEAR-STICKS

Gadgets, Guns, Gizmos and Gear-sticks

Ian Fleming understood the extraordinary attraction of 'things'. Not just material things (though Bond certainly appreciated those), but things that did things, for the 1950s was the great age of the machine: cars, domestic appliances, trains, planes, space-saving devices; machines to make life easier, faster and also, in the case of ever more sophisticated weapons, shorter. This was an age when domestic appliances – food mixers, teasmaids, televisions, fridges – were arriving in British homes in ever-increasing numbers.

Fleming adored gadgets. He was forever on the lookout for new inventions and new ideas, an interest reflected in his growing book collection with its emphasis on inventions and ideas that changed the world. When he took over the Atticus column at the *Sunday Times*, he rather pointedly changed the title from 'People' to 'People and Things'. His love of cars was legendary and, occasionally, life-threatening.

In his flat in Ebury Street he created a custom-made hatch, to enable the maid to serve food without being seen; in his bathroom, declaring a deep aversion to baths, he installed a modern shower (then a rarity) and a special soap dispenser. A customised object added a special glamour: after Bond proved a commercial success, Fleming rewarded himself with a gold typewriter, and even had a gold top made for his Bic biro. When describing technology or modes of transport in his books, Fleming worked hard to get the details right, and when he got them wrong (as he not infrequently did), he was grateful to readers for pointing out his mistakes. 'I take very great pains over the technical and geographical background to James Bond's adventures,' he wrote. His notebooks were filled with jottings on machines and gizmos he had seen or heard about. Whenever possible, he consulted experts. 'Facts,' he wrote, 'are clearer than people.' Minute technical descriptions have since become a stock in trade of the thriller writer, but Fleming was among the first to realise that readers (particularly male readers) have an almost insatiable desire to be told the precise make, size, shape and structure of every machine – even if the details are forgotten the instant they are read. Fleming both shared and fed this hunger for detail: the boat owned by the villain in *Thunderball*, Emilio Largo, is no mere luxury yacht but rather a hundred-ton hydrofoil adapted from the Shertel–Sachsenberg system, with a hull of aluminium and magnesium alloy, twin Daimler–Benz four-stroke diesel engines with Brown–Boveri turbo superchargers capable of fifty knots and costing £200,000. Some machines were imaginary; most were based firmly on reality, giving the reader the important sense of being told a fiction based on truth. Kingsley Amis called this use of real information in a fictional world 'The Fleming Effect', and it proved highly successful.

Secret service gadgetry – masterminded by the irascible Q – plays a crucial role in the James Bond films, reaching almost ludicrous levels of inventiveness with flame-throwing bagpipes, exploding toothpaste and invisible cars. But gizmos are also present in the books, courtesy of Q-Branch, the genuine wartime equipment unit under the extraordinary Charles Fraser-Smith. Based in a tiny office near St James's Park, Fraser-Smith commissioned some three hundred firms around London to make an array of ingenious gadgets. He called them 'Q gadgets', after the British warships disguised as merchant vessels known as 'Q ships' in the First World War. None of the things created by Fraser-Smith was quite what it seemed: a hairbrush containing a map and a saw; magnetised matches that doubled as makeshift compasses; a pipe lined with asbestos that could be smoked without destroying the documents hidden inside (though it might well destroy the smoker); invisible ink; miniature cameras hidden in cigarette lighters; a shoelace that could also be a handy steel garrotte. Fraser-Smith was one of the great unsung lateral thinkers of the war: he devised chocolate laced with garlic so that agents dropped into France might swiftly acquire pungent breath, the better to mix with the locals, and a screw-off button with a special left-hand thread in which miniature documents could be hidden. This, he believed, would take advantage of the 'unswerving logic of the German mind', since no German would ever think of trying to unscrew something the wrong way.

Fleming worked with Fraser-Smith, and his books are peppered with references to ingenious kit. Technological wizardry is not confined to Bond and his allies: his communist and criminal enemies have an equal share of the elaborate gizmos. In *Casino Royale*, Le Chiffre conceals 'Eversharp' razor blades in his hatband, shoe heel and cigarette case; a gun hidden in an innocent-looking cane is the first method employed to try to kill Bond; and a 'small carpet of steel spikes' is used to stop his car. When, in *Live and Let Die*, he heads to Mr Big's island, Bond has a full underwater equipment shopping list: 'Frogman suit complete with compressed-air bottle. Plenty of spares. And a couple of good underwater harpoon guns (the French ones called "Champion" are the best). Good underwater torch. A commando dagger . . . and some of the shark-repellent stuff the Americans used in the Pacific.' Plus a limpet mine and plenty of Benzedrine.

At various times, the Bond tool case included such necessaries as 'Luminous Readers' – special glasses which picked up the invisible ink used on playing cards – finger-print-powder spray, steel-capped shoes, the 'Inspectoscope' for airport inspections, a machine for the detection of contra-band using fluoroscopic principles, and an 'Identicast' machine to create a mock-up of Goldfinger's face. In *From Russia with Love*, Bond is kitted out with the full spy briefcase, a 'smart-looking little bag', containing: fifty rounds of .25 ammunition between the leather and the lining of the spine; fifty golden sovereigns in the lid; a flat throwing knife in each of the sides; a cyanide suicide pill in the handle (which Bond flushes down the loo); and a tube of Palmolive shaving cream – the top of which unscrews to reveal the silencer for his Beretta, packed in cotton wool. Bond uses a 'Homer' signal device planted in the tool compartment of Goldfinger's Rolls-Royce, and Goldfinger in return threatens to slice him up with a circular saw (which becomes a laser in the film).

Fleming's villains concealed weapons in the most unlikely places: a gun inside Tolstoy's greatest work; a .45 pistol disguised as a keyhole in Mr Big's desk; and Rosa Klebb's poison-bladed shoes (and knitting needles). Blofeld displays a lethal grasp of science, growing the castor bean plant, which is used to make ricin, a deadly poison favoured by terrorists today. Dr No has a flame-throwing jeep, and Oddjob, famously, a hat with a lethal metal rim. Compared to the extraordinary machines provided by Q in the later films, such gizmos may seem simple, but to Fleming's readers they represented the cutting edge of Cold War espionage technology.

The larger machines invented by Fleming also have a firm

base in reality. The Spektor decoding machine, which Tatiana Romanova promises to defect with in *From Russia with Love*, recalled the Enigma wartime encryption device (though the public would not learn of the 'Ultra Secret' until the 1970s). Drax's Moonraker missile was based on the German V-2 rocket bomb, the devastating missile deployed by Germany in the last stage of the war, which carried a ton of high explosive and had a range of over two hundred miles. Fleming later decided to give the threat even greater topicality by converting it into an intercontinental ballistic missile, which both the US and USSR were scrambling to develop at the time of the book's publication. Initially, the rocket is hailed as giving Britain 'an independent say in the world'; only later does Bond discover that it is aimed at London. The issues of nuclear deterrence and Britain's vulnerability gave the book a modern relevance that would only increase as the nuclear arms race gathered pace.

Since the Cold War was, to a large extent, a war fought between scientists on opposing sides, Fleming was determined to get the science right. He contacted numerous experts to ensure his fictional rocket came as close as possible to the factual object, writing to the British Interplanetary Society and even to Arthur C. Clarke, the doyen of science-fiction writers. Similarly, Fleming's fascination with the underwater world and the technology involved in deep-sea diving dates from his contact with one of the great underwater experts, Jacques Cousteau. Fleming first met Cousteau at a publishing party, when the French explorer invited the English author to visit him in the South of France, where he was then excavating the sunken remains of an ancient Greek ship. From boyhood, Fleming was driven, in his own words, by the 'raging desire to go somewhere and dig for buried treasure', and he was fascinated by the 'lonely and queer' underwater world Cousteau introduced him to. Two weeks spent scuba-diving and watching Cousteau's divers at work provided him with numerous details for later books. Most immediately, the extraordinary experience of loading up with thirty pounds of equipment and slipping into the 'limitless grey depths' furnished the technical inspiration for Bond's memorable underwater adventures in *Live and Let Die*, his second novel.

Fleming's crooks also display a firm grip on high technology – high, at least, by the standards of the time. Seraffimo Spang, boss of the Spangled Mob in *Diamonds Are Forever*, has a Cadillac with the windscreen ground to the precise prescription of his glasses; this may have enabled Spang to drive without spectacles, but imagine the experience for a passenger of seeing the road coming towards you through someone else's prescription lenses. Clearly the disinclination to wear glasses was some of sort of criminal affectation in Fleming's (myopic) eyes: Dr No wears contact lenses and so does Blofeld, in the latter case tinted dark green. Contact lenses were still a new invention, the first corneal lenses having been developed as recently as 1949. Dr No has an electric razor and a clock with luminous numbers; villains use walkie-talkies; the reader's attention is drawn to such technological luxuries as the seventeen-inch television in a Las Vegas hotel room, and the oxygen bar at Santa Fe airport. Today, such things seem fairly commonplace, but to readers of Bond in the 1950s they were marks of extreme technological sophistication. Bond, for example, drinks coffee made in an American Chemex. This was a one-piece, hourglass-shaped vessel of heat-resistant glass, an all-in-one coffee filter machine with a leather collar around its waist: the filter paper went in the top, and the coffee dripped through to the bottom. As a piece of domestic engineering, it was hardly complex, but it has since become a collector's item, displayed in design museums. The Chemex was invented in 1941 by a German chemist named Peter J. Schlumbohm (the sort of name that Fleming might have noted for future use). Very few readers today would know what a Chemex is; very few readers, in fact, would have known in 1955. But Fleming had tested and tasted coffee from a Chemex. It sounded modern and scientific, and it still does; and that, perhaps, is the point.

In May 1956, Fleming received the sort of reader's letter he partly dreaded and partly appreciated: James Bond, the writer complained, 'has a rather deplorable taste in firearms'. This was not, perhaps, all that surprising, since Fleming, unlike his brother Peter, had little time or taste for guns. He still owned the Colt .38 Police Positive engraved and presented to him by Bill Donovan, the US spy chief, but there is no evidence he ever fired it. He found the minutiae of gun science extremely boring, but as an essential element of the Bond mystique he appreciated the importance of accuracy. The letter-writer was one Geoffrey Boothroyd, a thirty-one-year-old ICI technician from Glasgow and an amateur firearms enthusiast of remarkable expertise. Boothroyd had an enormous personal collection of firearms in every shape and size, and an encyclopaedic grasp of the subject. The Beretta pistol Bond had used in the books so far was 'really a ladies' gun, and not a really nice lady at that', Boothroyd informed Fleming. In *Casino Royale*, Bond uses a Beretta in a chamois leather holster; Fleming himself had been issued with a .25 ACP Beretta during the war, and may have assumed it was the standard-issue secret agent's weapon; more likely it was simply the first gun he could think of.

Bond would be far better off, Boothroyd suggested, with a chunky Smith & Wesson .38 Centennial Airweight, a real 'man-stopper', carried in a Berns-Martin Triple-Draw holster with a built-in spring for rapid drawing. In addition, Bond should have a .357 Smith & Wesson magnum to keep in the car for shooting villains who might be further away. Fleming wrote back with polite enthusiasm, saying that Bond would certainly be pleased with his updated armoury, and adding, 'I am most anxious to see that he lives as long as possible and I shall be most grateful for any further technical advice.' There followed an extraordinarily arcane discussion about silencers: Boothroyd was against them, on the grounds that they are really the stuff of fiction. That, of course, was exactly why Fleming wanted to silence Bond's gun, and he claimed that he had used a silencer on a Sten gun during the war, which reduced the noise to a mere click. Fleming could not really care less whether a silencer worked in reality, but he needed it to work in fiction for the sake of his plots. Eventually, on Boothroyd's advice, Bond swapped his Beretta ('I am killing the bloody gun in my next book – on sound grounds') for a Walther PPK 7.65, because Boothroyd thought it was the best automatic of its size with ammunition available worldwide. With Boothroyd's help, the villains of SMERSH were kitted out, fictionally speaking, with 9mm Lugers and Mauser 7.63 automatics. Fleming swiftly got over the belief that guns were dull, and under Boothroyd's tuition became something of an expert: a staggering array of artillery is deployed in the Bond books, each described with full specifications, including a long-barrelled .45 Colt Army Special, a Savage 99F, a Winchester International Experimental .308 target rifle and a number of spear guns. Scaramanga, of course, totes a gold–plated single-action Colt .45.

Boothroyd loaned Fleming his own Smith & Wesson .38, which the artist Richard Chopping used as a model for the cover of *From Russia with Love*. Fleming's promise that this would make Boothroyd's gun 'for ever famous' was only a slight exaggeration, since the effect on its owner was exactly that. In *Dr No*, 'Major Boothroyd' is the name given to the secret service armourer, along with a flattering encomium from M: 'You may not know it, 007, but Major Boothroyd's the greatest small-arms expert in the world.' In the films, the characters of Q and Major Boothroyd are melded together, appearing in every film except *Live and Let Die* and *Casino Royale*. Boothroyd was now for ever famous.

Fleming's interest in machines found its most extreme (and expensive) expression in his love of cars. He wrote, and avidly read, motoring journalism, fell in love with cars passionately and promiscuously, and penned the most famous book about a car ever written: *Chitty Chitty Bang Bang* – published in 1964, the year of his death. Fleming himself owned a diverse succession of cars, from humble bangers as a young man to the magnificent black Ford Thunderbird he bought when he was famous, a car Ann Fleming considered 'above our price bracket and below our age range', which was probably why Ian loved it. Fleming was barely out of his teens when, on a long stretch of empty road near Henley, he reached 100 mph in a 3-litre Bugatti. At the age of twenty-two he bought a smart, black, two-seater Buick, in which he toured the Continent, developing a lifelong affection for the motoring holiday. From the black Buick he moved to a red Graham-Paige, then to a Morris Oxford, then to a 2.5-litre black Riley.

For a man who wrote with such relish about the thrill of driving fast, and boasted of the times he had exceeded 100 mph, Fleming rather surprisingly became a stickler for road safety, and campaigned for road signs to make the dangers more apparent. A 'motorcyclist trying to break the sound barrier . . . is aiming a loaded gun from the moment he leaves the garage', he declared. Though he wrecked his Thunderbird in 1961 after driving into an ice-cream van, Fleming was himself a good and restrained driver, which is more than can be said of Bond, who exhibits all the symptoms of road rage – shouting 'Silly bastard!' when forced to overtake on the inside. In Fleming's expert hands, cars became a form of costume for the players in the drama. While Drax drives his German Mercedes, Blofeld is to be found behind the wheel of a vulgar red Maserati, and Goldfinger luxuriates in his vast, gold 1925 Rolls-Royce Silver Shadow, an overweight monster of a car which must have been hell to drive without the invention of modern power-steering. If the villains' cars represent power, wealth and a certain cruel sophistication, then the cars driven by the Bond women are pure sex: Tracy di Vincenzo's Lancia Flaminia Zagato Spyder gives off a 'sexy boom' as she guns its engines. Domino Vitali drives a natty blue MG in *Thunderball*, while Tilly Masterton steers a grey convertible Triumph TR3. Fleming was conflicted about women drivers. In a typically sexist way, he thought that women tended to chat and lose concentration in cars, and considered a woman behind a wheel to be 'a mild hazard'. When Bond arrrives in New York in *Live and Let Die*, he is amazed by the number of women drivers in America. On the other hand, Bond himself finds nothing, except a gunfight, more exciting than 'being passed at speed by a pretty girl'.

Just as he relied on experts to help him with the details of guns and rocketry, so Fleming recruited technical assistance to organise Bond's garage, namely Aubrey Forshaw, the head of Pan Books and a connoisseur of large, fast cars. Bond's first car is the battleship-grey 1933 4.5-litre Bentley convertible with French Marchal headlamps and Amherst Villiers supercharger. This last modification was a characteristically generous plug for a friend: Amherst Villiers was a highly successful engineer who went on to become a painter, executing an excellent portrait of Fleming himself. When working on *Chitty Chitty Bang Bang*, Fleming asked Villiers to design a car that was 'really snazzy-looking to excite the imagination of children', thus forming a link between Bond's first car and Fleming's last. Bond bought the Bentley, we are told, 'almost new', in 1933, cherished it throughout the war, and services it with doting care. Indeed, his relationship with the car is rather more loving than with most of his women: he 'drove it hard and well with an almost sensual pleasure'. Bond's taste for Bentleys can be traced back to 1930, when Fleming reported on the Le Mans 24-hour race for Reuters and witnessed the great Anglo-German contest between the 6.6-litre Bentley Speed Six and the 7.1-litre SS Mercedes-Benz. The great white Mercedes, driven by Rudolph Caracciola and Christian Werner, made a deep impression on Fleming, and the race is rerun in *Moonraker*, when Bond's Bentley is engaged in a thrilling race with Hugo Drax's Mercedes 300SL. Bond's Bentley is written off soon afterwards, but before long he is back behind the wheel of another, now a Mark II Bentley Continental (a mistake, he apparently meant a Mark VI), this one fitted with a Mark IV engine, Arnott supercharger and magnetic clutch: 'The Locomotive'.

Fleming also changed cars regularly. After a succession of Renaults and an unsuccessful Daimler, with money from the film rights to *Casino Royale*, Fleming decided in 1955 to splash out on an American car. While staying with American friends, he had been introduced to a peculiar motorised hybrid (or mongrel): the 'Studillac', a Studebaker with a Cadillac engine. Ian test-drove the car, hit 80 mph, and was pulled over by the American cops, something that never happened to James Bond. Sure enough, the Studillac duly screeches into *Diamonds Are Forever*, when Felix Leiter introduces the beast with the explanation: 'You couldn't have anything better than this body.' Fleming called the Studillac 'a bomb of a motor car'. Eventually he settled on the Ford Thunderbird, and waxed poetic about its sheer power: 'When, on occasion, you can do a hundred without danger of going off the edge of this small island, you have not only the knowledge that you have an extra 20 mph in reserve, but the feel of it.' Ann nicknamed him 'Thunderbird', not entirely without mockery.

Bond drives three different Bentleys in the books, and only one Aston Martin, in *Goldfinger*, yet this is the car with which he will be forever associated, thanks again to the films. Bond selects the Aston Martin DB3 from the secret service pool. One senses that Fleming considers the car a little ostentatious, since Bond's cover at the time is that of a flashy young buck: it is grey, and fully equipped with headlights that can change colour to provide disguise in the event of a night-time chase, a radio receiver, reinforced bumpers and a Colt .45 in a secret compartment. In the films, Bond's cars are fitted with every sort of device, starting in 1963 with a car phone (then the height of luxury and cutting-edge sophistication), and going on to include ejector seats, tyre-shredders, weapons systems, anti-pursuit mechanisms, and so on. Both Fleming and Bond took pleasure in modifying cars, and in *Chitty Chitty Bang Bang* Fleming invented the ultimate convertible. Yet both loved cars less for their accoutrements than for the pure pleasure of driving, the 'fine, deep exhaust note'. For Fleming, cars meant style and escapism; for Bond, the mighty Bentley is 'his only personal hobby'.

Fleming's knowledge of gadgets and machines was more than merely a boyish enthusiasm for technology. By anchoring his fiction in things he had seen, used, driven and researched, the author placed Bond firmly in a high-tech, glamorous reality. Readers could sense that just as Bond came from somewhere real, so the weapons he uses and the cars he drives have a provenance, albeit an exclusive one, in the real world. As a collector of facts and things and people, Fleming knew that the essence of excitement was to convince the reader of an underlying authenticity. 'I do take a lot of my plots from life,' he said. 'They are certainly bizarre, but they are also made up of real things.'

006

BOND GIRLS

Bond Girls

It is a mark of James Bond's cultural reach that, for better or worse, a 'Bond Girl' has attained a specific meaning in modern parlance, with either positive or negative connotations depending on your point of view (and, perhaps, your gender). A Bond Girl is beautiful, for sure, and sassy and sporty; she is also sexually available, and unlikely to make a fuss when killed off, either literally or metaphorically, at the end of the last instalment to make way for a new love interest. She tends to be good at one-liners, but less inclined to intellectual conversation. In the books, at least, Bond's women are often damaged, in need of male protection, and have some small physical flaw. Like Bond's cars, they are attractive commodities, subject to modifications and improvements, but they can also be exchanged for newer, faster models without much regret. The Bond Girl is a very specific postwar fantasy. Fleming had enjoyed an expansive sex life before the war, but the war had loosened sexual mores greatly. Here was a hero enjoying sex, not merely outside marriage, but effectively without responsibilities or guilt.

Sex does not play a part in the lives of Bulldog Drummond or Richard Hannay. Indeed, Bond is really the first major British thriller hero to have an active sex life. Bond's attitudes to women caused outrage, titillation and amusement in roughly equal parts: they made a generation of men and boys very overexcited, and a generation of feminists extremely angry. Bond saves the girl; the girl sleeps with him: it is a simple contract. But even those critics prepared to see Bond's bed-hopping for the fantasy it was found something chilly and unpleasant in Bond's sexual licence and emotional reserve. In the films, Bond's sex life attained levels of priapism that would merit serious medical attention or industrial supplies of Viagra in a real human being. Henry Chancellor has calculated that Bond sleeps with just fourteen women in twelve books, between 1953 and 1964, of whom only five disappear between one book and the next, compared to an astonishing fifty-eight conquests in the first twenty Bond films. Readers who liked the Bond women in the books looked askance at the parade of almost characterless beauties being loved and left in each successive film. The writer Anthony Burgess wrote that 'the girls in the Bond films tend . . . to be nothing more than animated centrefolds. In the books they are credible and lovable because of some humanising flaw.'

Bond's approach to sex grew directly out of Fleming's own distinctive attitudes to women, which in turn were shaped by the times he lived in, the class he occupied, and his own psychological and sexual preoccupations. Fleming might have been an easy lay, but he was not an easy man. He has sometimes, somewhat unfairly, been characterised as simply a seductive lounge lizard, a philanderer gathering sexual scalps. The truth is more complex. Fleming was certainly attracted to many women; they were attracted to him, and he knew it. His charm, wit, vulpine good looks, wealth, mysterious war record and slight air of melancholy were powerfully seductive. He had many love affairs, often with other people's wives, including those of close friends. This was not because Fleming had a particular penchant for adultery: divorce was less prevalent then, and adultery more common. Sometimes these affairs were long-lasting, but mostly they were not. An American acquaintance was struck by his apparently clinical attitude towards women: 'He got bored with them fast and could be brutal about it. He had absolutely no jealousy. He explained to me that women were not worth that much emotion. But with it all, he had an abiding and continual interest in sex without any sense of shame or guilt.' Certainly, he was more versed in seduction than courtship. 'The direct approach to sex has become the norm,' he told one interviewer. His own approach was direct to the point of bluntness. He would ask a woman, often on slender acquaintance or first meeting, to go to bed with him; if she declined, he would simply move on, unashamed, unresentful and unembarrassed, to the next potential seductee. He was successful as often as not – odds which he seemed to find perfectly acceptable. Sex was a sort of sport, and he favoured the scattergun approach. 'He looked on women as a schoolboy does. They were remote, mysterious beings,' said one family friend. 'You will never hope to understand them, but, if you're clever, you can occasionally shoot one down.' The women with whom he developed close relationships tended to be older, and more emotionally resilient.

Fleming was tremendously interested in sex. Indeed, he studied and pursued the subject, in theory and in practice, with the same avid interest he showed in gadgetry, rocketry, science and political skulduggery. He took a close interest in French pornography, and assembled an impressive personal collection of erotica, which he liked to show to visitors, particularly female ones. Flagellation, which amateur psychologists like to trace back to his beatings at school, held a particular fascination. A certain amount of jocular whipping and slippering appears to have formed part of his marriage, and there are several references to these practices in Bond. Agent 007 periodically threatens (or perhaps offers would be a better term) to spank various women, including, rather courageously, Miss Moneypenny. Not one of the women thus threatened seems remotely surprised, let alone offended, by the suggestion of sexual domination. More unpleasantly, Bond's apparently insouciant attitude to rape has long provoked debate. In *Casino Royale,* we learn of Vesper Lynd that 'the conquest of her body, because of the central privacy in her, would each time have the sweet tang of rape'. Worse yet, in *The Spy Who Loved Me*, the narrator Vivienne Michel opines: 'All women love semi-rape . . .' Fleming, under a barrage of criticism, tried to argue that *The Spy Who Loved Me* was an attempt to show young people that Bond was not a good role model. My own view is that Fleming was not seriously defending rape, or even semi-rape, but trying to shock by reinforcing the idea of Bond's essential cruelty. If so, he shocked far more than he intended, and he still does, leaving a tang of toleration for sexual violence that is very far from sweet.

Yet there was, as so often, another side to this careless sexual conquistador. Fleming's longer-term relationships were not with the cocktail party poppets and sexual silhouettes of the novels, but with older, married women. He cultivated the air of a roué, but he also longed for emotional stability. His relationship with his eventual wife Ann Rothermere (another wife of a friend, whom he married in 1952) was long, intense, complex and fierce, but also supportive and, at times, deeply loving. At one tempestuous juncture in their stormy marriage, he wrote to Ann: 'What we both want is more love and warmth but that is a fire we both need to blow on if it is to burn.' Bond could never have said that. Fleming was obsessed with women, but afraid of intellectual females (such as Ann) who might put him down. He was detached but also needy, admiring but distant. It is entirely possible that, for all his skirt-chasing, Fleming did not in the end like very many women, and understood even fewer. The novelist Rosamond Lehmann acutely observed: 'The trouble with Ian is that he gets off with women because he cannot get on with them.' He professed a cynicism he did not always feel. 'You can have love for nothing up to the age of forty,' he once observed. 'After that, you have to tell a story to get it.' This is a quite sad and self-revealing observation. Fleming undoubtedly broke some hearts, yet most of the women he slept with must have had a good idea of what they were (or rather were not) getting into. He was never deliberately cruel, and most of his lovers attest to his gentle, if detached, kindness. Clare Blanchard, a Wren whom Fleming met in Ceylon, told her brother: 'It doesn't make any difference that I don't mean anything to him as he's so awfully nice.'

As a young man, Fleming hopped from woman to woman with few regrets, except perhaps one. Muriel Wright was twenty-six, and a fresh-faced English rose, when Fleming met her in Kitzbühel in 1935. 'Mu', as he called her, was an expert rider, skied beautifully, and was one of Britain's foremost polo players. She came from the finest landed British bloodstock: her Old Etonian father had been an MP and a contemporary of Val Fleming. With an explosion of wild blonde hair that earned her the nickname 'Honeytop', she was also exceptionally beautiful, in an artless way, and refreshingly unconventional. She was rich enough not to have to work, but nonetheless made a good deal of money modelling sportswear and, almost scandalously, swimsuits on the beach at Monte Carlo. Muriel loved horses, dogs, parties, gossip and fun, but most of all she loved Ian Fleming, to the point of self-abasement. She would caddy for him on the golf links, and rush to collect his custom-made cigarettes when he ran out; she would come when he called, and stay away when he was seeing other women. One of his friends called her Fleming's 'slave'.

Ian enjoyed showing Mu off to his friends and annoying his family by introducing this slightly scatty beauty into weekend house parties. But he undoubtedly treated her very badly. Even though they were unofficially 'engaged', Fleming was consistently and relentlessly unfaithful to her, and, unlike some of his lovers, she minded. It is said that her lack of intellect stood in the way of his commitment, but then there is no evidence Fleming considered brains to be an attractive quality in a woman, and quite a lot to indicate otherwise. Fleming's reputation was well known to Mu's horrified family: they marked Fleming down as a bounder, and her brother Fitzherbert even turned up at Fleming's home with a horse whip, intending to administer the traditional punishment for cads, only to find that Ian and Muriel, forewarned, had headed off to the safety of Brighton for the weekend. For nine years, Mu obediently trotted after Fleming. She even got a job as a motorcycle dispatch rider working for the Admiralty when Fleming was with the Naval Intelligence Division.

Then suddenly, like some character in a Bond movie, she was dead. On 14 March 1944, Muriel Wright returned to her flat in Eaton Mews (having just delivered Fleming his weekly package of cigarettes) and went to bed. That night, there was an air raid: a chunk of flying masonry hurtled through her open window, striking Mu in the temple and killing her at once. Ian, as her only known contact, was summoned from the card table to identify the body. Fleming was distraught. He was also racked with remorse at the way he had treated her. He wore Mu's bracelet on his key ring and refused to go to the London haunts they had visited together. One of Ian's associates in 30 AU, Dunstan Curtis, remarked meanly of his mourning: 'The trouble with Ian is that you have to get yourself killed before he feels anything.' But, in truth, the death of Muriel had a profound effect on Fleming's emotions, a small effect on his behaviour, and far greater impact on his writing. Mu, he reflected sadly, had been 'too good to be true'.

The quality of being 'too good to be true' is, of course, what distinguishes the Bond Girls. Muriel Wright has a strong claim to be the *fons et origo* of the species: pliant and undemanding, beautiful but innocent, outdoorsy, physically tough, implicitly vulnerable and uncomplaining, and then tragically dead, before or soon after marriage. Bond would have married Vesper Lynd, in *Casino Royale*, but she kills herself. Ten books later, there are distinct elements of Muriel in the well-born, golden-haired Countess Teresa (Tracy) di Vicenzo, in *On Her Majesty's Secret Service*. Bond *does* marry Tracy ('She's beautiful, in bed and out. She's adventurous, brave, resourceful. She's exciting always'), but soon afterwards she, too, perishes. Bond's distress over Tracy's corpse may be an echo of Fleming's anguish at Muriel's death so many years earlier.

A year before he had met Muriel, Fleming first laid eyes on Ann (née Charteris), the young wife of Shane, Baron O'Neill, and future wife of Esmond, Lord Rothermere, and the woman Fleming would finally marry in the same year he wrote his first Bond book. Ann was in many ways the opposite of Mu, being dark, highly intelligent, waspish, worldly, sophisticated, emotionally complex and extraordinarily good company. Ian's love affair with Ann started during the war; it continued after O'Neill's death and her marriage to Rothermere; and it lasted, tumultuously, until the end of his life. This peculiar pair had very different tastes and interests: Ann enjoyed nothing more than to gather her literary and artistic friends for an evening of bibulous backstabbing, the sort of event that Ian cordially detested, preferring the golf course, the club, or simply his own company. Ian was hardly the marrying type. To a friend, newly betrothed in 1944, he remarked sourly, 'Well, old boy, I wish you all the luck in the world, but I can't see anything in it for me.' When Ian and Ann finally did decide to marry, on 24 March 1952, he was forty-three, she was pregnant, and he anticipated the worst. Writing to his future brother-in-law, he observed: 'We are, of course, totally unsuited . . . China will fly and there will be rage and tears.'

There were, indeed, ample tears and flying crockery. Ann could be wounding about Ian's writing (referring to it as 'pornography'); he, in turn, made no secret of his dislike of her literary friends, her 'harem'. After two years of marriage, he was already complaining, only half in jest: 'In the old days I demanded or perhaps pleaded for three things in a wife. She should have enough money to buy her own clothes, she should be able to make incomparable Béarnaise sauce, and she should be double-jointed. In the event I got none of these things.' The rows grew furious, and the marriage colder. Fleming conducted a long affair with a neighbour in Jamaica, Blanche Blackwell; Ann did the same with Hugh Gaitskell, leader of the Labour Party. She was jealous; he, characteristically, was not. When they were apart, they missed each other painfully, he declaring: 'I love you only in the world.' When they were together, they fought viciously and, as self-absorbed people often do, publicly. Many of their friends thought the marriage should have broken up, but somehow it did not; paradoxically, the repeatedly adulterous Fleming was wedded to the idea of matrimony. Fleming wrote every one of his Bond books while locked in this peculiar relationship, in an extraordinary torrent of creativity. Perhaps Bond was a way to escape the pains of his marriage. Once he had started writing, and suffered the sneers of Ann's literary friends, he may have been impelled to keep going in order to prove that he could out-write, out-publish and out-earn every one of them; perhaps as he felt his sexual powers waning, he poured his passion into his books, for his love of words and writing was the most constant love of his life. Whatever the reason, this strange marriage endured, producing one child, Caspar, a few good times, some very unhappy times, and a lot of excellent books.

It is tempting to see shades of Fleming's turbulent marriage in Bond's attitude to women. The 'conventional parabola' of a Bond affair, described in *Casino Royale*, is a statement of unalloyed cynicism, starting with 'sentiment, the touch of the hand', and inevitably ending with 'the final bitterness': 'The meeting at a party, the restaurant, the taxi, his flat, her flat, then the weekend by the sea, then the flats again, then the furtive alibis and the angry farewell on some doorstep in the rain.' Bond has no time for domesticity and marriage, 'handing out canapés in an L-shaped drawing room' – a reference to the Flemings' London house in Victoria Square. Bond points out that if he got married, he would first need to divorce himself from M and the secret service. James Bond has no children, no siblings and no parents. He leaves Kissy Suzuki pregnant in *You Only Live Twice*, but there is never a suggestion that he has any sense of paternal responsibility, or wonders about his child. He is the empty vessel into which the reader decants his or her expectations. Women, Bond declares, are for recreation; he has no desire to tote the emotional baggage that comes from a serious relationship. Tracy, the girl he does marry, is eligible precisely because she is 'a lone girl, not cluttered up with friends, relations, belongings', rather like himself. Bond's women often have interesting, independent lives and missions; they are by no means chained to the sink, but essentially they are there to be admired, saved and then slept with, in that order. Even a lesbian like Pussy Galore melts before Bond's male dominance: 'She did as she was told, like an obedient child.' Bond is adamant on one point of female gastronomy: the ideal woman needs to make a Béarnaise sauce as well as she makes love, though not, presumably, at the same time.

The qualities Bond admires are physical and practical, and certainly not a matter of character or intellect: 'Gold hair. Grey eyes. A sinful mouth. Perfect figure. And of course she's got to be witty and poised and know how to dress and play cards . . .' Fleming was something of a connoisseur of women's fashion, and often describes the clothing of Bond's lovers in lavish detail. The wit is an interesting requirement, since the Bond of the books is never remotely witty: the jokes and one-liners are purely inventions of the films. Fleming uses a great many adjectives to describe the shape of women's breasts most admired by Bond, foremost among which is 'jutting'; this quality, however, is not so attractive when associated with the buttocks, as is the case with Tatiana Romanova's overexercised and therefore unattractively masculine bottom. Elsewhere, confusingly, Fleming approvingly describes a female bottom as 'boyish', a description that sent Noël Coward into a paroxysm of fake-heterosexual outrage: '*Really*, old chap, what could you have been thinking of?' Other critics have got very hot under the collar at Bond's sexual activity: 'Sex, Snobbery and Sadism,' screeched Paul Johnson in the *New Statesman*, blasting the 'mechanical, two-dimensional sex-longings of a frustrated adolescent'.

Fleming worked hard on his seduction technique, but Bond barely needs one: women simply throw themselves at him. Bond Girls are all, of course, intensely attractive, but each bears some small imperfection, a mark of vulnerability: Honeychile Rider has a broken nose; Domino Vitali has one slightly shorter leg. Even their names usually offer the hint of availability, and were often drawn from people Fleming knew: Honeychile was the nickname of Pat Wilder, an American former dancer in Bob Hope's troupe who married Prince Alex Hohenlohe, owner of an exclusive Alpine resort where Fleming went to ski and socialise; Jill Masterton is a play on the name of John Masterman, the Oxford academic who presided over the Double Cross system of double agents during the war; 'Solitaire' (Simone Latrelle in *Live and Let Die*) is named after a unexpectedly dowdy Jamaican bird.

Bond is pure heterosexual, from his brogues to his haircut (which cannot quite be said of Fleming, who had many gay friends and could be fantastically camp). 007 does not approve of homosexuals ('unhappy, sexual misfits') or sexual equality, or even votes for women. His books, Fleming declared, were 'written for warm-blooded heterosexuals'. Outside of the more Jurassic corners of London clubland, it would be hard, these days, to find anyone with the same views as James Bond. 'Doesn't do to get mixed up with neurotic women in this business,' M tells Bond gravely in *From Russia with Love*; 'They hang on to your gun-arm.' All of this adds up to a very potent postwar daydream for a particular sort of old-fashioned gent. Women had the vote and there was nothing even Bond could do about that. Having played a vital role in the war, women were asserting themselves in the home and the workplace; they were even becoming secret agents, and had been effective as such during the war, being rather better in that line of work than men. Male dominance was under threat wherever one looked, but not in Bond's world. Bond offered a reassuring fantasy, old-fashioned in tone but modern in sexual liberty: men were still the world's heroes, modern Saint Georges who could slay the dragon and then fall into the arms of an adoring, beautiful, slightly weak woman, who would love them unquestioningly and then whip up a terrific dinner. Why, he could even cause the toughest lesbian to declare, as does Pussy Galore: 'I never met a man before.'

To many modern men, the Bond Girl myth is still a powerful fantasy; for many modern women, to be called a Bond Girl would be an unforgivable insult. Perhaps that shows that we have not moved on so very far since 1955. Now, woman, where is my Béarnaise sauce?

007

SHAKEN, STIRRED
AND CUSTOM-MADE:
BOND'S LIFE OF LUXURY

Shaken, Stirred and Custom-made: Bond's Life of Luxury

'There are moments of great luxury in the life of a secret agent,' Ian Fleming declared in the opening line of *Live and Let Die* (1954). It is almost impossible to exaggerate the allure of Bond's lifestyle to a postwar Britain strained by rationing, deprived of glamour and still bruised by the privations of war. Bond is, quite simply, a stylish, fast-shooting, high-living, sexually liberated advertisement for all the things ordinary Britons had never had, yet dreamed of: the finest food and drink, smart clothes, fast cars, leisure time, casinos, exotic foreign travel, swimming in warm waters. Fleming called his evocation of this fantasy 'disciplined exoticism'. But he was also one of the first writers to identify the appeal of the designer lifestyle in an emerging age of consumerism. Identifying Bond with certain brands made him not only classy, but believable.

Fleming had history on his side, for his dealings in

wartime espionage had shown him that spies do, indeed, enjoy and require moments of great luxury. Much spycraft is boring, dangerous and uncomfortable, and spies tend to be self-interested people, fascinated by material things. Perhaps because of this, human comforts and luxuries assume a disproportionate importance when an agent is off duty. John Masterman, organiser of the famed Double Cross system through which Britain played Germany's spies against their German spymasters, held it as an article of faith that secret agents should be pampered and cosseted, provided with money and, within the bounds of reason and tight security, allowed to indulge themselves with whatever comforts were available. Popov, the Yugoslavian agent who spied for Britain throughout the war, was encouraged to live the life of a gambling, hard-living playboy (not that he needed much encouragement); Eddie Chapman, codenamed Agent Zigzag, was given the 'red-carpet treatment' by his MI5 handlers, wined and dined at the Savoy, and allowed to spend the money he had brought from Germany on wine, women and, to a slightly lesser extent, song. In framing Bond's life of exquisite good taste and effortless style, Fleming must surely have been thinking back to the refined wartime spies he had known, like Biffy Dunderdale, who drove around Paris in his Rolls while France collapsed, and dined at Maxim's in his tailor-made suit.

Bond never has to wait in for the electrician or arrange

to see the bank manager. He never queues for a bus. In almost every way, his imagined life was entirely divorced from the everyday realities of 1950s Britain. Yet there were people in postwar Britain living a life of exclusive, stylish luxury, and one of them was Ian Fleming. 'I write about what pleasures and stimulates me,' he said, 'and if there is a strong streak of hedonism in my books it is not there by guile but because it comes through the tip of my ball-point pen.'

From an early age, Fleming had enjoyed the good (and expensive) things in life: skiing in the Alps, dining at Scott's, membership of the most exclusive clubs for gentlemen and golfers. For most of his life, however, he did not have quite as much money as he would have liked, and when he did have that kind of money towards the end of his life, having earned vast quantities from his books, it was too late. There is a hunger in the way Fleming describes gold, diamonds, a villain's den or a delicious meal that transmits itself to the reader as a sort of luxurious longing. Many of his acquaintances were super-rich, most notably his schoolfriend Ivar Bryce, a charming and handsome Anglo-Peruvian sybarite whose already vast family fortune from trading guano was increased immeasurably when he married Jo Hartford, an American supermarket heiress whose fortune was worth an estimated $350 million. The Bryces had homes in, among other places, Manhattan, Vermont, London and the Bahamas (where they had a property complete with a fake beach, imported at $3,000 a yard); they bred racehorses, travelled constantly, partied hard and lived a life of quite breathtaking extravagance. Fleming could be disparaging about the rich, claiming that too much money left millionaires in 'search of identity'; on the other hand, he would have been more than happy with the identity of a multimillionaire himself. His villains are almost all fabulously wealthy: money, and the power it can buy, is central to their evil fascination. 'Too much money is the worst curse you can lay on anyone's head,' Bond tells Marc-Ange Draco in *On Her Majesty's Secret Service*. If so, it was a curse Fleming pursued with consistent determination, and remarkable success.

Fleming was never in the same financial league as the Bryces, but he was still a great deal wealthier than most people, and thanks to a generous expense account provided by Kemsley Newspapers he could live a life that was rather richer than he was. As a young man, he perfected a sort of roué bachelor-chic that lasted throughout his life. He wore suits of the fashionable cut, sported a spotted bow-tie, or the Old Etonian tie ('The colours are really quite unobjectionable'); Fleming considered his tie-wear 'Churchillian'. Churchill did favour spotted black and blue bow-ties (he had only six other ties in the 1950s), which he tied loosely, a style copied precisely by Fleming. Through a long and elegant ebony cigarette holder, Fleming sucked a never-ending succession of custom-made cigarettes. Fleming's smokes were Morland Specials, a tar-heavy confection of strong Turkish and Balkan tobaccos, each one decorated with three gold bands around the filter, in reminiscence of the three gold rings he had worn on his sleeve as (acting) Commander Fleming of the Royal Navy. Bond smokes the same brand, sixty a day and seventy if he is gambling, but when abroad he will smoke whatever the locals are puffing: Chesterfield King Size in the US, Royal Blend in the Caribbean. Fleming's cigarettes were a curious affectation, and a lifelong addiction, but they were also the mark of a man who knew the value of standing out from a crowd. He wore Trumper's 'Eucris' hair dressing (which Bond also uses in *Diamonds Are Forever*), collected rare books and disdained tea, the working man's drink – Bond declares it 'mud'. Bond's dark suits, Fleming noted with a flash of introspection, 'betray an underlying melancholy'.

On the beach in Jamaica, Bond wears bright beach shirts made by Antonio's of Falmouth, but for everyday wear he sports a blue Sea Island cotton shirt and tropical worsted trousers. Bond and Fleming share most sartorial tastes, although 007 favours black knitted silk ties and would not, I suspect, be seen dead in a spotted bow-tie. Quite how he obtains his wardrobe is a mystery, since Bond goes shopping just once in fourteen books. Little flickers of the more old-fashioned side to Fleming's character occasionally shine through: Bond, for example, takes against anyone wearing a tie knotted in the Windsor style, which he considers 'a mark of vanity, egocentricity and a pawky mind'. (In Red Grant, it is also the mark of an assassin.) Behind Bond the fashion icon lurks Fleming the harrumphing, old-school patriot, disapproving of vulgar dressers, bad manners and homosexuals (even though two of his closest friends, William Plomer and Noël Coward, were gay). Some of Bond's fashion choices would be considered disastrous today, but were then a mark of extreme sophistication, and all reflected Fleming's own idiosyncratic fashion: Bond's taste for pyjama-coats, for example, and black leather sandals (we are not told whether he wears socks with these, but I prefer to assume not).

Fleming's sense of style undoubtedly reflected, in part, his friendship with and admiration for Somerset Maugham. The two writers had met in 1953, when Maugham was already a grand old man of letters, living a life of elegant private luxury in his stunning villa on the Côte d'Azur, with plenty of servants, rare works of art and a sumptuous library. Fleming was deeply impressed by Maugham's expensive English lifestyle.

In some ways Goldeneye, the Jamaican holiday home he purchased in 1946, would become Fleming's answer to Maugham's Villa Mauresque: a haven dedicated to pleasure but also to the hard grind of daily writing. Fleming first visited Jamaica back in 1942, when he travelled there for an Anglo-American naval conference, accompanied by

Ivar Bryce. He was immediately smitten by the place. 'When we have won this blasted war, I am going to live in Jamaica,' he declared. 'Just live in Jamaica and lap it up, and swim in the sea and write books.' To another friend he announced that he would never spend another winter in Britain. On the north shore of the island, he found the property he was looking for, on the site of an old race track, facing the sea, with a secluded private beach. Once more, there was wordplay in the holiday home he called Goldeneye: a reference to the wartime planning for the defence of Gibraltar, Operation Golden Eye, but also a tribute to the Carson McCullers novel *Reflections in a Golden Eye*, which he happened to be reading at the time, and to the original Spanish name of the place, Orcabessa, 'head of gold'. Here Fleming would retreat from the fogs and gloom of wintry London to entertain his friends, snorkel in the warm blue waters of the reef, relax in private luxury and, eventually, write. When it was time to leave this sanctuary in the spring and return home (usually with another finished manuscript in his briefcase), Fleming would always do so with 'a lump in the throat'. Bond would come to share Fleming's deep affection for Jamaica, and in *Live and Let Die* we learn that 007 'had grown to love the great green island and its staunch, humorous people'.

Bond's style is an exaggeration of all the elements that Fleming believed made up the essence of English *savoir-vivre*, with a lot of contemporary consumer goods and designer products thrown in for added glamour. In some respects – most notably food – Bond is far more of a connoisseur than Fleming himself was, but once again he knew instinctively that readers demanded detail. It is not enough to know that Bond wears an expensive watch; we need to know it is a Rolex Oyster Perpetual (although, as Fleming told a reader, he 'has trained himself to tell the time by the sun in either hemisphere within a few minutes'). He does not smoke any old thing (except when abroad), but keeps his Morland cigarettes in a gun-metal case and lights them with a Ronson. He does not simply eat, he eats magnificently and in exquisite detail. Bond's grooming is precise almost to the point of prissiness. His hair is washed in Pinaud Elixir ('that prince among shampoos', he insists, camply), he washes his body with Fleur des Alpes soap by Guerlain, and shaves with a Hoffritz razor. Bond, in short, is a highly perfumed fashion icon, with a licence to smell lovely. 'My books are spattered with branded products of one sort or another,' Fleming remarked nonchalantly, but these designer goods are as vital to the man as his machines, his guns or his women.

Bond is a foodie; indeed, he may be the first action-foodie-hero in the thriller genre. Fleming's suggestion that Bond, when not on assignment, often dines simply (grilled sole, *oeufs en cocotte* and the like) stands in sharp contrast to his gastronomic behaviour throughout the series. In

Casino Royale, Bond declares from the outset: 'I take a ridiculous pleasure in what I eat and drink.' He puts this gourmandising down to being a single man who must often eat alone. Bond's first blow-out, consumed with Vesper Lynd, is worth examining in some detail, for it says much about his tastes (and Fleming's literary intentions). They eat caviar and toast (lots of toast), followed by rare steak tournedos with Béarnaise sauce (so we know what is coming, bed-wise) and artichoke hearts; then Vesper has strawberries and cream, while Bond eats an avocado pear with French dressing. To drink, they have a bottle of the Taittinger Blanc de Brut 1943 – 'probably the finest champagne in the world', Bond muses, and then grins 'at the touch of pretension in the word'.

A touch? To modern ears, this may not sound like a particularly sumptuous meal, but to postwar readers it was almost impossibly recherché and luxurious: a rare, tiny steak when meat itself was rare, usually rubbery and often semi-cremated; an avocado pear was a singularly exotic delicacy – so uncommon, in fact, that Bond seems to think it is a pudding. Champagne is already glamorous enough: the ability not only to spot the difference between one champagne and another, but to declare one to be supreme, that would have been, for Fleming's readers, the mark of true connoisseurship. Pretentious? That was the point: here was a banquet of such immense refinement and expense that readers would be left salivating.

The same is true of many Bond meals. He eats yoghurt in Turkey, but not the low-fat variety; his is 'deep yellow with the consistency of thick cream', and some fresh figs, peeled and 'bursting with ripeness'. This, of course, was in the days before fresh yoghurt could be found in every supermarket in the world. In France, Tilly Masterton is told to buy Bond's lunch: 'Six inches of Lyon sausage, a loaf of bread, and half a litre of Mâcon with the cork pulled.' A bottle of wine with the cork still in it would be merely frustrating, but the precision is the point. Drawing on Fleming's worldwide travels, Bond scoffs every possible gourmet item: lobster in Japan, a doner kebab (then almost unheard of in Britain) in Istanbul, stone crabs and pink champagne from silver tankards in *Goldfinger*, turbot *poché*, *sauce mousseline*, and half a roast partridge from the restaurant opposite the train station in Etaples run by Monsieur Bécaud. For breakfast (his favourite meal, and Fleming's), Bond eats boiled eggs from Maran hens (three and a half minutes each), eaten off Minton china, with toast, Wilkin & Sons Tiptree 'Little Scarlet' strawberry preserve, Frank Cooper's Oxford Vintage Marmalade, honey from Fortnum & Mason, and coffee from De Bry in New Oxford Street, brewed, of course, in the Chemex. The culinary name-dropping is intense: sole meunière, tartare sauce, eggs Benedict, thousand island dressing. With M, in the fictional Blades Club, Bond eats asparagus with hollandaise sauce; in Scott's he feasts on lamb cutlets

Fleming smoked custom-made Morland Specials, each one decorated with three gold bands in memory of the rings on the sleeves of the wartime naval uniform. He smoked elegantly, constantly and fatally.

Ernst Stavro Blofeld (played by Donald Pleasence), Fleming's arch-villain, pictured here with his white Persian cat, an accoutrement that never appears in any of the books.

Aleister Crowley, occultist, mystic, drug addict and sexual omnivore, was the 'wickedest man in England', according to his detractors. He may also have been the inspiration for Le Chiffre, the villain of *Casino Royale*.

MR ERNO GOLDFINGER

Ernö Goldfinger, the modernist architect, who was so enraged to see his name appropriated by Fleming and attached to a gold-obsessed super-crook that he threatened to sue.

Courtesy of Times Newspapers Ltd

Commander Lionel 'Buster' Crabb, the naval war hero whose headless body was found more than a year after he was sent by MI6 to inspect the hull of a Soviet cruiser – provoking a political furore and inspiring the plot of *Thunderball*.

Nikolai Khokhlov, still hairless from the effects of radioactive poisoning caused when his coffee was laced with thallium – a revenge attack eerily reminiscent of the more recent murder of former KGB officer Aleksandr Litvinenko.

Geoffrey Boothroyd (*left*), the firearms expert who advised Fleming to re-arm James Bond with something more manly than his Beretta. He was rewarded by having his name attached to 'Major Boothroyd', Fleming's fictional secret service armourer.

Sean Connery and Ian Fleming in the film set of *Dr No*, 1962.

Eva Green and Daniel Craig as Vesper Lynd and James Bond in the 2006 film of *Casino Royale*, the biggest box-office hit for Bond so far.

)ger Moore with film producers Cubby Broccoli (*right*) and Harry Saltzman on the roof of the orchester Hotel in London.

Desmond Llewelyn as Q, the Einstein of the espionage gadget, with Pierce Brosnan in *Golden Eye* (1995).

Images on this page courtesy of EON Productions

Prototypes of Rosa Klebb's famous dagger-shoes, as worn by Lotte Lenya in the 1963 film of *From Russia with Love*: elegant, and lethal.

Bullet-holed cello from *The Living Daylights*.

Spear guns from *Thunderball* (1965).

Fleming makes scrambled eggs: twelve eggs, lashings of butter, then some more butter. 'I think you sometimes add cream instead of the last piece of butter', he wrote. Note his unconventional 'hotplate'.

Bond in the bunker: Ian Fleming playing golf.

GK 3841

Ian Fleming poses by a Bentley, similar to Bond's first car, the battleship – grey 1933 4.5-litre Bentley convertible he drives in *Casino Royale*.

Fleming at the card table. 'The same cries of victory and defeat, the same dedicated faces, the same smell of tobacco and drama. For Bond, who loved to gamble, it was the most exciting spectacle in the world.' (*Moonraker*)

with buttered peas and new potatoes, and a slice of pineapple. To modern, sophisticated palates this is unextraordinary fare, but to contemporaries Bond's meals are bright explosions of high cuisine, specifically designed to tantalise and amaze in a Britain where bananas were considered mouth-wateringly exotic, milk came powdered, and practically everything tasted the same and of very little. In 1948, with control over food supplies even stricter than it had been during the war, the average man was rationed to two ounces of bacon and ham, one and a half ounces of cheese and two ounces of tea each week, and just one egg every five days. The memory of deprivation was still fresh in 1953, and meat rationing would not end until 1954. Bond's diet of asparagus, fresh lamb and pineapple *in a single meal shows* just how far above the average he is.

But here is a small heresy: James Bond might be the ideal comrade in a fight, but in a restaurant he would be sheer hell. Bond would be forever ordering *for* you, offering a little lecture on the wine or champagne, or insisting, as foodies always will, that you cannot eat at the nearest brasserie but must instead trek all the way over to the station in Etaples to try Monsieur Bécaud's divine turbot *poché*. Bond would be the sort to pick a fight with the chef and sommelier. He would forever be on the lookout for Béarnaise sauce. Anyone who insists that food tastes different off Minton china is, in my view, a pain. I am not alone in this. Fleming himself would surely have found

Bond a tiresome dining companion: the writer knew the literary value of exotic and complicated foreign food in fiction, but he was no gourmet in fact. Few writers are better at describing food, but eating was not a subject that interested Fleming greatly.

At one point Fleming notes that Bond, when abroad, prefers 'the ordinary plain food of the country'. This was certainly true of Fleming, whose eating habits were closer to M's than to Bond's. His own tastes were straight out of the prep school recipe book. Mostly, he liked scrambled eggs, which 'never let you down', and he did not care much what kind of hen they came from. He insisted that the chef at the Lutèce in New York, then one of the most expensive and exclusive restaurants on the planet, prepare for him scrambled eggs (then strawberries for dessert). Fleming even wrote out his own recipe for scrambled eggs, which offers the artery-clogging suggestion that a meal for four should consist of twelve eggs, six ounces of butter, and additional butter to be stirred in after cooking. However, the food Fleming served at Goldeneye – violent goat curries and the like, prepared by his Jamaican house-keeper Violet – was famously revolting, a far cry from the delicacies served by Somerset Maugham at the Villa Mauresque. Noël Coward wrote that 'the food was so abominable I used to cross myself before eating it . . . it tasted like armpits. And all the time there was old Ian smacking his lips for more and you are tormented by the thought of all those exquisite meals in the books.' Regardless of the quality of the food he served and ate, Fleming was by all accounts a delightful dining companion, entertaining, inquisitive and attentive, particularly if you happened to be an attractive woman. Bond to choose the food and wine, and Fleming to eat it with: that would be the ideal dinner.

'He is basically a hard liquor man,' Fleming said of his fictional creation. 'He is not a wine snob.' Put rather more basically, Bond will drink anything if it is exclusive and sophisticated, and he does, in sometimes quite astonishing quantities. Indeed, his intake of alcohol is so prodigious on occasion that it is amazing he can still stand, let alone shoot straight or make love. In *Moonraker*, before playing cards with Drax, Bond manages to put away a vodka martini, a carafe of vintage vodka from Riga, a bottle of Dom Pérignon champagne and half a packet of the drug Benzedrine. He does not stop there: this is followed by a large brandy and then another entire bottle of champagne. It is something of a relief to discover that Bond is not immune to hangovers. The next morning he vows: 'Champagne and Benzedrine! Never again.' Benzedrine is the trade name for racemic amphetamine, a form of artificial stimulant which causes euphoria, heightens the senses and suppresses the appetite. 'Bennies' were among the first synthetic drugs to be used recreationally, and Benzedrine was used by bomber crews during the Second World War and later by soldiers in the Vietnam War. The socialite 'Chips' Channon used to put it in the cocktails he served during the war, to ensure his parties went with a bang.

In the films, Bond's drinking is essentially pared down to three specific drinks: vodka martinis ('shaken, not stirred'), champagne and whisky on the rocks. In the books, however, his drinking habits are far wider. Bond has a 'head like a rock', according to M, which is just as well given the alcoholic pounding it gets. In *Goldfinger* we find Bond 'luxuriating in the peace and heat of the whisky'. At times, he seems to be less luxuriating in alcohol than marinating in it. As in everything else, Fleming is careful to furnish brand names whenever possible and, like the best barmen, he keeps the drinks coming in a steady stream. As the series developed, readers came to expect an ever more extensive drinks menu. In *On Her Majesty's Secret Service*, for example, the eleventh book, Bond downs no less than forty-six drinks, the widest variety in any single book. According to one Bondologist, these include: unspecified quantities of Pouilly-Fuissé white wine, Taittinger champagne, Mouton Rothschild '53 claret, calvados, Krug champagne, three bourbons with water, four vodka and tonics, two double brandy and ginger ales, two whisky and sodas, three double vodka martinis, two double bourbons on the rocks, at least one glass of neat whisky, a flask of Enzian schnapps, Marsala wine, the better part of a bottle of fiery Algerian wine (served by M), two more Scotch whiskies, half a pint of I. W. Harper bourbon, a Jack Daniel's Tennessee whisky with water, on the rocks, a bottle of Riquewihr wine, four steins of Franziskaner beer, and a double Steinhäger gin. The same indefatigable researcher has found that although vodka martini has now become Bond's signature drink, he only drinks nineteen of them in the books, compared to thirty-seven bourbons, twenty-one Scotches and a remarkable thirty-five sakes (entirely the result of his massive consumption of that particular drink in *You Only Live Twice*).

In the first book of the series, Bond specifies that his martini must be shaken: 'shaken, not stirred' has since become perhaps the most immediately familiar catchphrase of them all, a required element in every Bond film (except when it is deliberately omitted or parodied). Martini drinkers have long debated whether a vodka martini is better shaken or stirred (and even whether a vodka martini is really a martini at all); the theory appears to be that, if shaken, the martini gets colder than if it is simply stirred. That fits in with Bond's requirements: 'I never have more than one drink before dinner. But I do like that one to be large and very strong and very cold, and very well made.' In fiction, Bond's insistence on shaking over stirring is yet another example (along with food, wine, and women) of how 007 is discriminating, sophisticated and has extensive insider-knowledge of the drinks cupboard.

In common with his gastronomic explorations, Bond

tends to drink the alcohol native to the country he is in: raki in Turkey, sake in Japan, bourbon in Kentucky. Vesper Lynd is the heaviest drinker among Bond's lovers, drinking twice as much as any other 'Bond Girl'. But the villains drink practically nothing, except Drax, who has just four drinks in *Moonraker* while Bond polishes off eighteen. This is not as curious as it seems. Today we associate heavy drinking with a lack of self-control. No latter-day hero could be seen to stick away the tidal wave of booze consumed by Bond, and his drinking has steadily tailed off in the movies in line with modern mores. But to Fleming, clubbable and convivial, drinking meant relaxation, ritual and reliability. A teetotaller was not quite a man to be trusted.

Fleming's own drinking was less varied than Bond's, but just as voluminous, and far more damaging. He made no claim to wine connoisseurship (for the oenophile details he consulted experts, as usual). In Moscow, as a young journalist, he picked up a taste for vodka, but gin and dry vermouth was his habitual tipple. He even wrote an article for visiting Americans, offering guidance on how to order a decent martini in an English pub. During the war, he was steadily putting away a bottle of gin a day. When his doctor warned him this was doing him no good, Fleming switched to bourbon, favouring a brand called Old Grandad. When writing, he would not drink at lunchtime but started at sundown, with a long succession of martinis, whiskies or bourbons. He would pause during dinner, and then resume thereafter. Fleming came from a hard-drinking generation, and there is no known incident of his embarrassing himself or behaving drunkenly. The heavy drinking and relentless smoking doubtless shortened his life, but that was his choice, and his lifestyle, and at least some of that rubbed off on his creation. To censure Fleming and Bond for their unhealthy lifestyles is, of course, ludicrous. Fleming certainly did not censure himself, and nor did he feel any need to modify his intake: 'I will not waste my life trying to prolong it,' he once declared. Given his habits of consumption, Bond ought to have been a halitotic, wheezing, impotent, bronchial, leathery and obese poster boy for the perils of drink and tobacco; but he is not, and that is perhaps part of the Bond miracle.

Though he may have kicked off the Bond books by describing the rank stench of a casino in the early hours of the morning, Fleming loved to gamble and so, of course, does Bond. Again, for most contemporary readers, the evocation of a casino, however sweaty, brought glamour, money and the faint whiff of sin. Gambling in casinos or any 'common gaming house' had been illegal in Britain (except in private clubs) since 1854, and its gambling laws would not be relaxed until 1960. Fleming had developed a taste for the card table as a young man about town before the war, when he and his more rakish friends would sometimes fly to Le Touquet or Deauville for a weekend of gambling, golf and girls. Those experiences, and his wartime visit to the casino at Estoril in Portugal, would help inform the memorable scenes in *Casino Royale*. Fleming was fascinated by the theory of gambling and the mentality of the wealthy and reckless gambler: as a young man he brushed shoulders with the so-called Greek Syndicate, a group of ship owners who ran the casino at Deauville. The syndicate's most remarkable dealer was Nicholas Zographos, a character whose stony coolness of temperament matched that of Bond himself. Fleming, unlike Bond, was a cautious gambler, and often an unsuccessful one. Bridge was his game, and although he developed into a good player, he lacked the patience and mathematical precision to master the art beyond amateur competence. At first he played at Boodles, and later at the Portland Club, where the stakes were higher: the two clubs would be amalgamated to form the 'Blades Club' in *Moonraker*, in which Fleming devotes more than sixty pages of intense and vivid description to the game.

Indeed, Fleming became something of an advocate for gambling. For the *Sunday Times* he wrote an article entitled 'How to Win at Roulette with only £10', which was turned down on the grounds that its racy tone might not sit well with the more prim consciences among the newspaper's readership. But it was precisely the sense of indulging in forbidden fruits that gave Bond, the best gambler in the British secret service, such cachet. In journalism, as in fiction, Fleming knew well how to conjure up 'the noisy abracadabra of the roulette table', a heady species of magic most of his readers could barely imagine. By setting scenes in casinos (a literary device borrowed from Somerset Maugham), Fleming transported his readers away from the bomb-scarred cities of Britain to a brighter, sweeter and thrillingly degenerate world. In a semi-serious article for the *Spectator*, entitled 'If I Were Prime Minister' (a fairly alarming proposition), Fleming suggested that the Isle of Wight be turned into a huge pleasure island, where 'frustrated citizens of every class could give rein to the basic instincts for sex and gambling which have been crushed through the ages'. (Given his earlier suggestion that the Isle of Wight be made French during the war, one wonders what Fleming had against this blameless island.)

Fleming's other main recreational hobby was golf. It may seem strange, in an age when golf is one of the most democratic and widely played games in the world, that at the time when Bond was first climbing into his plus-fours the sport held a peculiar, elite glamour. Fleming first played golf with his grandmother, took up the game at prep school, and played until the end of his life (indeed, a cold caught playing golf led to his final illness). It was a game that gave him the purest and simplest pleasure, and most weekends he could be found on one of Britain's courses: Gleneagles, Cooden in Sussex, and most famously at Royal

Saint George's in Kent, which would become the fictional Royal Saint Mark's in *Goldfinger*. Golf offered Fleming the sort of male companionship he often craved, the opportunity to spend a few hours in the open air with some like-minded, clubbable friends, a modicum of exercise followed by an immodicum of drinks. Once again, his enthusiasm outpaced his ability: he played off a handicap of nine (so does Bond), but developed an inhibiting 'flat swing' (so does Bond). Agent 007 is happy to cheat his way to victory in *Goldfinger*, something his creator would never have done (even if his opponent was already doing so), but Fleming was also happy to gamble on the outcome: when he was young, the bet was a mere £1; as he grew older and richer, the stakes rose to a hefty £50 a round or more. Fleming never became a golf bore, because while he was passionate about the game he never took it too seriously. Sometimes the wager was frivolous – say, a pair of monogrammed pyjamas. He scandalised the stuffier members of the Old Etonian Golfing Society by presenting it with an unusual prize cup: a chamber pot inscribed with the words 'The James Bond All Purpose Grand Challenge Vase'. He was also capable of mocking his own golfing pretensions, as in an article entitled 'Nightmare among the Mighty' which he wrote for the *Sunday Times* about his participation and unexpected success in a pro-celebrity tournament.

Swimming had been a passion of Fleming's since

boyhood, a form of relaxation he could enjoy even more after the acquisition of Goldeneye. Fleming was a strong swimmer, and the sea had always fascinated him. He passed his halcyon memories of childhood bucket-and-spade holidays on to Bond, who reminisces about the 'painful grit of wet sand between young toes when the time came for him to put his shoes and socks on, of the precious pile of sea-shells and interesting wrack on the sill of his bedroom window . . . of the small crabs scuttling away from the nervous fingers groping beneath the seaweed in rockpools'. This is the closest Bond ever gets to nostalgia. With the help of Jacques Cousteau, Fleming glimpsed the extra-ordinary underwater riches, and his daily swim and snorkelling along the reef at Goldeneye became part of a beloved ritual. He made an in-depth study of the fish in the lagoon, and bound it in black leather. Though no fan of the hunt on land, he chased barracuda with a spear gun in the shallower waters, and once went shark hunting, using a dead animal carcass as bait, an experience he described as the most exhilarating of his life.

Ian Fleming spent much of his life behind a desk – at the Admiralty, at the *Sunday Times* and at Goldeneye – and the rest of his time trying to escape from the confines of a desk-bound life. He was a permanently restless man, constantly on the alert for the next exciting or interesting location he might like to visit, and bring into his fiction. Fleming was always a dedicated tourist and, usually, someone else paid the travel bills: Reuters in his youth, the Royal Navy during the war, and Kemsley Newspapers in later life. This restlessness and love of movement was transmitted directly to Bond, who is constantly trying to prise the 'blubbery arms of the soft life' from his throat and beat back the boredom of London life by hitting the road on his next assignment. Once again, Bond's travels to distant and exotic locations, on an apparently limitless expense account, represented a level of expenditure and freedom beyond the dreams of most readers. Even though foreign holidays and air travel were becoming a possibility for ordinary people, restrictions on the amount of money one was allowed to take out of the country still made foreign travel exceedingly difficult for most.

Bond travels to America and the Caribbean, to Switzerland and the Seychelles, to Turkey, Canada, Japan and France. Usually he travels by plane – air travel in the 1950s was expensive, luxurious and time-consuming – and reflects: 'If I ever married I would marry an air hostess.' Wherever he goes, the weather is wonderful. 'The sun is always shining in my books,' Fleming remarked. Conversely, in Bond's Britain, the weather is reliably horrible, cold, windy and miserable, or else unpleasantly sweltering. This is the place that Bond and his readers escape from. It is easy, and even a touch galling, to imagine Fleming sitting at his desk in Jamaica, opining on the horrors of an English winter while looking out over the azure waters of his private tropical lagoon. 'Yes,' reflects Major Smythe in *Octopussy*, '[Jamaica] was paradise all right, while, in their homeland, people munched their Spam, fiddled in the black market, cursed the government and suffered the worst weather for thirty years.'

If the books occasionally read like travel brochures, that is because Fleming regarded himself, in some measure, as a travel agent, a proselyte for the delights of foreign parts with a duty to reveal new and different worlds to his readers. His particular powers of observation and description made him a natural travel writer. He actively promoted Jamaica as a holiday destination for sun-starved Britons, declaring: 'English people should become Empire-minded for their holidays.' Only one Bond book, *Moonraker*, the third in the series, is set entirely in Britain. The evocation of Kent reflected Fleming's love of that county, but the decision to restrict Bond to home turf prompted complaints from some readers keen to be transported elsewhere; thereafter, Fleming sent Bond abroad in every novel.

Wherever Bond travels, Fleming has travelled first. As with all his writing, the fiction is firmly anchored to facts, people and scenes he had experienced at first hand. He wrote with his travel brochures, notebooks, postcards and other travel memorabilia on the desk beside him. Sometimes he disguised and fictionalised reality, but often he did not.

'I see no point in changing the name of the Dorchester to the Porchester,' he said. At times, the detail is so precise that Bond begins to sound like a travel adviser from the AA: watch out, warns 007, for 'the dangerous crossroads where Le Touquet's quiet N38 meets the oily turbulence of the major N1'. This is the travel equivalent of the Amherst Villiers supercharger in Bond's Bentley, the *sauce mousseline* on his turbot, and Domino's attractive limp: the devil, and the delight, is in the detail.

Fleming's taste for travel was established in his youth with his sojourns in Europe, surely exacerbated by Peter's success as a travel writer, then consolidated by his wartime wanderings, and finally thoroughly expanded by his indulgent employers in peacetime. The *Sunday Times* gave Fleming a virtual licence to travel at will, a long rein that would be unheard of in newspapers today, and was pretty rare even then. In 1959, the features editor, Leonard Russell, approached Fleming with the sort of suggestion that newspaper editors, in my experience, never make: would Fleming care to take a five-week, all-expenses-paid trip around the world, to visit the globe's most thrilling cities? Astonishingly, Fleming apparently needed persuading to take up this offer. 'Surely you want to pick up some material for your stories,' said Russell. 'It's a wonderful opportunity.'

Fleming's 'Thrilling Cities' world tour in 1959 was a remarkable odyssey. The first leg took him to Hong Kong ('modern comfort in a theatrically oriental setting'), Macau, to gamble in a nine-storey house of pleasure, and to Tokyo, where he composed haikus with geisha girls. In Hong Kong he linked up with the *Sunday Times* Asia correspondent, Richard Hughes, a large and ebullient Australian (and part-time spy) who was doyen of the city's foreign press corps, and in Tokyo he was guided by another journalist, 'Tiger' Saito. As with Nazim Kalkavan, his Turkish guide to Istanbul in 1956, Fleming would repay his local guides by granting them immortality in *You Only Live Twice*, as Richard Lovelace 'Dikko' Henderson, the Australian stationed in Japan, and Tiger Tanaka, the head of the Japanese secret service. Fleming was no culture-vulture; his requirements were entertainment, comfort and colour: 'No politicians, museums, temples, Imperial palaces or Noh plays, let alone tea ceremonies.' He wanted to experience casinos, restaurants and brothels, the high life, night life and low life, the glamour and, of course, the girls: 'In the East, sex is a delightful pastime totally unconnected with sin,' he declared. But then, sin had never been much of a preoccupation for Fleming.

The plane from Tokyo to Hawaii caught fire and nearly crashed. In Los Angeles, he visited the head of police intelligence to bone up on the local mafia scene, and in Las Vegas he made $100 on the slot machines and stole three ashtrays as souvenirs. In Chicago, he broke his own no-museums rule and visited that city's fine collection of

Impressionist art, but he also found time to see a striptease ('positively exquisite boredom') and the site of the St Valentine's Day Massacre. New York, his final destination and a city he had always loved, proved, on this occasion, to be a disappointment, no doubt compounded by travel fatigue after more than a month on the road and his mounting ill health. Fleming complained that the city was in thrall to television and tranquillisers, and in a later Bond short story he grumbled that the best restaurants had been colonised by a new 'expense account aristocracy' – a criticism which, given his own elevated position within that particular caste, was pretty rich. Some of this jaundiced attitude to America would reappear in *You Only Live Twice*, when Bond reflects on Britain's fast-diminishing global role and Tiger Tanaka hits out at the new American superpower dominating East and West: 'Baseball, amusement arcades, hot dogs, hideously large bosoms, neon lightings.' Just a few months later, Fleming would repeat the 'Thrilling Cities' experience with a whistle-stop canter through selected European cities, including Hamburg, Berlin, Vienna, Geneva (where he met Charlie Chaplin) and Monte Carlo.

These trips would result in a successful and popular newspaper series covering thirteen cities in all. 'Thrilling Cities' was published in book form in 1963, but beyond that the extended double journey furnished Fleming with vast amounts of contemporary material for his novels. Ann remarked acidly that she did not see how Ian could be thrilled by any city, since he never stayed long enough to see anything. But that was the way Ian travelled, Fleming wrote and Bond lived: impressionistically, thrillingly and very fast.

Travel, golf, swimming, gambling, reading, book-collecting: these were all, to some extent, the habits of a solitary man. The boy who had eschewed team games at Eton in favour of athletics remained a solo player all his life. The character traits that made him shy away from commitment to women were also those that drove him to pursue, alone, the things that most fascinated him. This surely also explains why, in that explosion of creativity in the last years of his life, he was able to devote himself utterly to the most solitary and lonely occupation of all: writing.

Bond's lifestyle echoed and exaggerated that of his creator, perhaps to a greater extent than any other twentieth-century writer, though the parallels are far from perfect. Bond is a superb shot, whereas Fleming hated shooting, and did it as seldom as he could. Bond exercises daily, and retains his fitness despite his habits, while the summit of Fleming's health regime was swimming or an amble around the golf course. Fleming was an avid reader, book collector and bibliophile; Bond's bookshelves are apparently full, but there is little evidence he has ever read the books therein.

Indeed, books are hardly mentioned in Bond's world, save for a few, including *Hogan on Golf*, *Scarne on Cards* and a few books written (inevitably) by Fleming's friends: Raymond Chandler, Eric Ambler and Patrick Leigh Fermor, as well as JFK's *Profiles in Courage*. Bond lives in Chelsea and never has the slightest money worries; Fleming, until the final chapter of his life, never had quite enough cash. Bond reads *The Times*, every day; Fleming, a journalist to his core, read every newspaper and magazine he could lay his hands on. Bond is childless and parentless; Fleming had a complex relationship with his mother, and strove to be a good father to his only son, Caspar. Fleming was brought up in an age where children were to be seen and not heard; in Bond's life they are neither seen nor heard.

Fleming had not intended to give James Bond a style. He was to be a blunt instrument, an empty vessel. But in the end, in spite of himself, Bond's way of life and way of thinking were broadly those of Fleming. Above all, Fleming and Bond share an interest in things, the rarer and more exclusive the better. In this, both writer and creation were harbingers of a new consumer age, when lifestyle and fashion would matter increasingly, and the label often proclaimed the man. 'We are the only two writers,' Fleming told Somerset Maugham, 'who write about what people are really interested in: cards, money, gold and things like that.' Bond admits, almost sheepishly, to taking a 'ridiculous' interest in food, drink and other material things. But Fleming knew exactly what he was doing. The writing technique he pioneered was far from being ridiculous, and very close to being inspired.

THE SHORT LIFE
OF IAN FLEMING; THE
ETERNAL LIFE OF JAMES BOND

The Short Life of Ian Fleming; The Eternal Life of James Bond

By 1961, and the publication of *Thunderball*, James Bond is ailing. As the book opens, he wakes up feeling dreadful, chronically hungover. Boredom, and the soft life he has always feared, are taking their toll. M dispatches him to a health farm, Shrublands, where the medical report is stern. 'The officer's daily consumption of alcohol is in the region of half a bottle of spirits of between sixty and seventy proof,' the doctor writes. 'The tongue is furred. The blood pressure a little raised at 160/90 . . . the officer admits to frequent occipital headaches.' The report blames Bond's habits: 'I believe these symptoms are due to the officer's mode of life. He is not responsive to the suggestion that over-indulgence is no remedy for the tensions inherent in his professional calling . . .'

Fleming's report on the health of his hero was broadly autobiographical: the drinking, high blood pressure and

headaches were all symptoms suffered with increasing persist-
ence by the writer himself. In Bond's refusal to countenance
changing his unhealthy and indulgent lifestyle, Fleming was
stating his own determination not to waste his life by trying
to extend it. Yet he was aware that his body was failing.
Shrublands is based on Enton Hall, an expensive and exclusive
health farm, or 'hydro', in Surrey. Ann Fleming had visited
Enton Hall, and she persuaded Ian to book into the health
farm to treat his painful sciatica, headaches and generally
failing health. He did not enjoy the strict regime, and scoffed
at the faddish nature remedies prescribed. His doctor
prescribed more pills.

For all his vigour, Fleming had never enjoyed robust good
health. The shadow of mortality was seldom far behind him,
and in a notebook he wrote with wry candour: 'I've always
had one foot not wanting to leave the cradle, and the
other in a hurry to enter the grave, which has made for an
uncomfortable existence.' Fleming was just thirty-eight when
he first began to suffer serious chest pains, which spread to
his neck. A New York medical specialist told him to cut
down on the cigarettes and drink, advice that he would
continue to receive, and fail to heed, for the rest of his life.
He suffered from stress and persistent headaches – possibly
a legacy from his broken and ill-mended nose. A cardiogram
in 1949 showed no evidence of heart disease, but in retrospect
what Fleming called the 'iron crab' had plainly already taken
a grip on his heart. In 1956, he was struck down by agonising

kidney stones, which would develop into another recurrent problem. Soon after the publication of *Thunderball* in 1961, Fleming suffered a major heart attack and spent a month in hospital, followed by a long convalescence at a hotel on the coast near Brighton. He was put on a strict diet, which he tried to circumvent by sneaking in smoked salmon and other forbidden delicacies. He also began writing *Chitty Chitty Bang Bang*, based on the bedtime stories he would tell his son Caspar. 'There is not a moment even on the edge of the tomb,' he told his publisher, 'when I am not slaving for you.'

He joked that Ann was trying to convince him that 'going for long walks and looking for birds' nests is the right way to spend the next forty years of my life'. Fleming had just three years of life left, and for all his grim joviality, he probably knew it. Blanche Blackwell, his lover in the final few years, noted that he was 'fighting like a tiger to live, but everything was against it'. *Thunderball* opens on a bleak note: 'It was one of those days when it seemed to James Bond that all life, as someone put it, was nothing but a heap of six to four against.' For Fleming, the odds on his own life expectancy were steadily getting worse, but at the very moment when his books were about to hit the most astonishing winning streak.

When describing his writing methods, Fleming reached for a water-sports metaphor: 'Each chapter is like a wave to be jumped as we race behind the hero like a water-skier behind a fast motor boat.' Forcing the reader to turn the page was the only rule of thriller-writing that mattered, and he stuck to the formula religiously, writing at the pace of the most daredevil water-skier, but with iron discipline. Over the course of fourteen years, every one of the Bond novels was written in Goldeneye as winter turned to spring, usually taking about eight weeks, and then published a year later: two thousand words every morning between 9.30 and 12.30, or approximately seven hundred words an hour. 'If you interrupt the writing of fast narrative with too much intro-spection and self-criticism, you will be lucky to write five hundred words a day,' he advised.

There spoke the true journalist. Unsurprisingly, he some-times made mistakes: occasionally the plot blows a gasket, and screeches to a halt; sometimes the narrative flags; and the later Bond books lack some of the brio of the early novels. But for the most part, the books sail along with infectious verve and confidence. Returning to England with a completed manuscript, Fleming would then set to work correcting the proofs of the book written the previous spring, before starting to cook up a fresh plot, with new experts and fresh opportunities for travel. It was a hurtling rhythm of work, and it translated into a breathless, heart-thumping style. For Fleming, the demands were exhilarating, exhausting and relentless. He seldom rewrote in any substantial way: the books seemed to flow from him almost fully formed, on the initial draft. The first people to see the manuscript would be William Plomer, Fleming's old friend and his most loyal and reliable critic, and his brother, Peter. The self-deprecation continued: 'My books are straight pillow-book fantasies of the bang-bang kiss-kiss variety,' Fleming declared, with that appealing nonchalance. This was simply untrue. Fleming had discovered an extraordinary recipe, and the public, if not always the critics, recognised it as such.

The reviewers, at least initially, were gentle with James Bond. When not plugging the work of his friends in newspapers or novels, Ian was an avid and expert self-promoter, and as a senior newspaperman he was in a position to ensure some favourable notices; yet the rave reviews were more than mere log-rolling. With the publication of *Casino Royale*, the *Sunday Times*, his own newspaper, hailed Ian Fleming as 'the best new thriller-writer since Eric Ambler'. But other newspapers, which might have been expected to be more impartial or even hostile, were equally enthusiastic: 'Ian Fleming has discovered the secret of narrative art,' declared John Betjeman in the *Daily Telegraph*. 'Don't miss this,' advised the *Observer*. Even the *Times Literary Supplement*, bible of the higher-browed, proclaimed: 'Mr Fleming has produced a book that is both exciting and extremely civilised.' Amid all the plaudits, however, one can already detect the early rumblings of the backlash that would eventually follow. One reviewer considered the scenes of torture in *Casino Royale* 'too monstrous to be excused'. Another recommended that Fleming 'cut down on the physical violence'. The reaction to the US publication was also somewhat muted. In one of the more remarkably askew assessments in literary history, one reviewer insisted that this British secret agent was 'passé'.

The first print run of *Casino Royale*, 4,750 books, sold out in a month. Jonathan Cape, the publisher, had not expected much from the book, and agreed to accept it for publication only after Peter Fleming, an established author, interceded on his brother's behalf. 'He's got to do much better if he's going to get anywhere near Peter's standard,' Cape remarked. But with *Casino Royale* selling well, Cape offered Fleming a contract for three further books, and his career as a novelist was well and truly launched. James Bond, as ever, provoked different reactions: some serious-minded critics baulked at the implausibility; others squirmed at the sex and violence; a few resented the brand-naming and what looked like product placement, as it has since become known. But Fleming also found supporters in the most unlikely and useful places. He had been introduced to Raymond Chandler at a luncheon party given by the poet Stephen Spender. The acclaimed master of the American detective novel would prove a loyal fan, reviewing both *Diamonds Are Forever* (apparently his first ever review) and *Dr No*, and declaring Fleming to be 'probably the most forceful and driving writer of what I suppose still must be called thrillers in England'.

Sales were good, but nowhere near what they would become, or what Fleming would like them to have been.

Some of Fleming's early success may be ascribed to canny promotion, and some to mere good luck. If *Live and Let Die* had been entitled *The Undertaker's Wind*, as Fleming originally planned, then one wonders if the entire Bond series might have come to a premature end. Reviews for the first five books were, on balance, positive. In Fleming's own words, 'the great thing is that each one of the books seems to have been a favourite with one or another section of the public, and none has yet been completely damned'.

Damnation, swiftly followed by the breakthrough Fleming craved, would come in 1958 with the publication of *Dr No*. The critics rounded on Fleming, almost as a pack, and Bond-bashing became the order of the day. Fleming's writing was pilloried as vulgar, licentious and immoral, snobbish and anachronistic, with a nasty flavour of sado-masochism. The most famous assault came from Paul Johnson in the *Spectator*, who claimed that Bond had been cooked up from three base ingredients: 'all unhealthy, all thoroughly English – the sadism of the school bully, the mechanical two-dimensional sex-longings of a frustrated adolescent, and the crude, snob-cravings of a suburban adult'. The London literary cognoscenti had always looked down on Bond, even, most painfully for Fleming, his own wife Ann and her coterie of writers and intellectuals, which included such luminaries as Evelyn Waugh and Peter Quennell. Ann could be particularly withering, refusing to allow him to dedicate *Casino Royale* to her on the grounds that 'books of this sort' (i.e. cheap ones) do not merit dedications. 'I would so love him to triumph over the sneers of Annie's intellectual friends,' observed Noël Coward. And triumph he did. The attacks reflected the fact that Fleming was now well known enough to warrant being attacked: helped by the notoriety and controversy, the faint but exciting whiff of immorality and sexual mischief, the Bond books acquired their own momentum. The critics continued to complain, often savagely; the readers, too, were sometimes angered when Fleming appeared to tinker with the established formula, as in *The Spy Who Loved Me*, narrated by the fictional Vivienne Michel. But Bond was becoming unstoppable. In 1959, *Goldfinger* hurtled directly to the top of the best-seller lists.

Fleming knew the value of a plot twist, but nothing could have prepared him for the change in Bond's fortunes that would occur when 007 finally transferred to the movie screen. In October 1962, Fleming attended the film premiere of *Dr No*, the first instalment in what would become the most valuable cinematic franchise in history. Bond, for better and for worse, would never be the same again. Nor would he ever again be solely the product of Fleming's imagination. For many people, James Bond is a film character (or several film characters), but his path to the screen had not been simple or swift. Fleming had always intended that his creation should transfer to film or television, and as with the books, he worked hard to bring about the transformation.

This was less easy than, with hindsight, might have been

expected. The rights to *Casino Royale* were sold to CBS in 1954 for $1,000 and later adapted into a television play as part of a series entitled *Climax*, now almost wholly forgotten. Sir Alexander Korda, the great Hungarian-born producer, toyed with the idea of making *Live and Let Die*, but the idea came to nothing. In 1958, Fleming was commissioned to write a thirteen-part Bond series, again for CBS in the US. Once again, the project foundered, but much of the material Fleming had written would be recycled in different forms in the later books. Like many writers, Fleming was frustrated by Hollywood's capacity for encouraging talk and no action: 'hollow bonhomie combined with ultra-sharp horse-trading' was how he put it. Yet he persevered, and set out to create a film project of his own. Through Ivar Bryce, he met an up-and-coming filmmaker, Kevin McClory, and together (along with screenwriter Jack Whittingham) they set about writing a treatment for an underwater Bond adventure set in the Caribbean. Once again, the project foundered, mainly for lack of financial backing, but as usual Fleming was unwilling to see hard work go to waste and adapted the idea into the novel *Thunderball*. This time, however, the recycling got him into serious trouble, when McClory and Whittingham claimed the book was based partly on their work and sued in the High Court for breach of copyright. The resulting legal wrangle was bitter, intensely complex and, for Fleming, quite debilitating; it would not be resolved for a further thirty-seven years. At one point in the process, he was reduced to drawing up a list of the ideas, details and inspirations that he had put into the book, in order to back up his claim to sole authorship. This legal document again demonstrated both the depth and eclecticism of Fleming's research: the specifications for the *Disco Volante*, for example, had been obtained from the Italian boat manufacturer Leopoldo Rodriguez;the title *Thunderball* came from a conversation in which Fleming had heard this term used to describe an American atomic test; and so on. For later archaeologists of the Bond phenomenon, such details are fascinating; for Fleming, forced to pick apart his own writing in order to prove ownership, the entire legal experience was hellish. His first heart attack came just two weeks after the court action was launched. 'I do not think James Bond would be at home in the Chancery Division,' Fleming observed morosely as the case dragged on.

Film salvation arrived in the somewhat unlikely double act of Albert Romolo 'Cubby' Broccoli, an experienced Italian-American Hollywood producer, and Harry Saltzman, a Canadian former circus performer and intelligence agent turned movie impresario. Saltzman had acquired the film rights to all the Bond books (save *Casino Royale*), and in partnership with Broccoli he founded EON Productions – standing for Everything Or Nothing – which was a good motto for their high-stakes gambling style. United Artists signed up to make six films, with Fleming earning an impressive $100,000 per film and 5 per cent of producer's profits. Broccoli and Saltzman decided to open the franchise with *Dr No*, which has arguably the most filmic of the Bond villains. Bond was about to hit the big time on the big screen, but Fleming's control over the character, inevitably, would begin to diminish.

It is said that Fleming initially wanted the part of Dr Julius No to be played by Noël Coward, his old friend and neighbour in Jamaica, a prospect that would have been hilarious, and probably disastrous. He also suggested that David Niven, another friend, should play Bond, or Richard Burton, whom he much admired, or else a young actor named Roger Moore. Ian's suggestions were politely ignored, though in private Broccoli could be less than flattering about the novelist's work: *Dr No*, he allegedly said to one potential director, was 'full of nonsense'. Cary Grant was initially offered the part of Bond, but at fifty-eight he declined, reportedly saying he was too old for the role. Eventually Broccoli decided to cast Sean Connery, an almost entirely unknown Scottish actor who had previously worked as a truck-driver, life-class model, milkman, coffin polisher, sailor, boxer and lifeguard. Fleming had lunch with Connery at the Savoy, but wondered if this Scottish working-class 'overgrown stuntman' was quite right for the part. His doubts were allayed when an attractive woman at the same lunch assured him that Connery had 'it', the indefinable sex appeal that would work on screen. Even if he had objected, it is doubtful whether Fleming's opinion would have made much difference: under the terms of the contract, he had no influence over or input into the scripts. In any case, as screenwriter Richard Maibaum conceded, there was an 'untransferable quality' in the novels. Fleming's role was restricted to scouting film locations in Jamaica, but there is no evidence he minded: like many sensible authors, he decided to bank the cheque, stand in the wings and watch the action from a discreet distance.

Even so, Fleming became predictably fascinated by the mechanics of film-making, and he had a clear notion of how Bond should be presented on screen. As in the books, he believed Bond should be depicted as a 'blunt instrument wielded by a government department', a cog in a 'tough, modern organisation', and not particularly appealing 'until [the audience] get to know him and then they will appreciate that he is their idea of an efficient secret agent'. In the end, however, the screen Bond was very different from Fleming's version. For a start, he was a great deal more promiscuous, and substantially more bloodthirsty. The literary Bond is prey to doubts and occasional uncertainty: life as a licensed killer 'is a confusing business', he admits on paper, but never on screen. In print form, Bond is capable of introspection, even as he goes about his hard-hearted business. 'I never intended him to be a particularly likeable person,' Fleming wrote, but in the films Bond is not only instantly and enduringly attractive, but charming and, above all, amusing. The one-liners became a staple feature of Bond in his film incarnation (the less funny his quips, paradoxically, the better), but in the books the brooding Bond is almost entirely devoid of humour. Fleming himself could be witty and wry, but deliberately did not pass on those qualities to Bond, the better to preserve the 'ironical, brutal and cold' character within. Fleming's Bond, unlike his film counterpart, is capable of fear, mistakes and pain. When his plane is tossed by a storm in *From Russia with Love*, Bond retreats, in his terror, into the impregnable 'hurricane room' at the centre of his personality. (Once again, Fleming himself had experienced the raw terror of flying through a storm in a plane in the 1950s.) On screen, Bond never suffers from such human frailties.

There have been six Bond actors to date, and each successive Bond has evolved the character in different, sometimes contradictory, directions. Connery (1962–7, 1971 and 1983) was determined, rugged, effortlessly sexual; George Lazenby (1969) laconic, humourless and perhaps closest to Fleming's Bond; Roger Moore (1973–85) was jocular, suave and playful almost to the point of parody; Timothy Dalton (1987–94) gritty, serious and occasionally reluctant to accede to the demands of the job; Pierce Brosnan (1994–2002) witty, charming, athletic; Daniel Craig (from 2005) blond, humane and remarkable in swimming trunks. Countless arguments, several fights and no doubt a number of serious doctoral theses have been devoted to the issue of which actor made the best Bond. Indeed, the debate has been going on so long that it has become one of those cultural signifiers: if you are over fifty, and used to smoke, you are likely to be a Connery-Bond fan; if you are between forty and fifty and have ever worn a car coat unironically, then you will plump for Roger Moore; if you were born after the fall of the Berlin Wall, then Daniel Craig is, for you, the only true Bond. It may be a cliché to say that every age gets the Bond it deserves, but to an extraordinary extent the character has proved a cultural weathervane, reflecting the evolution of fashions, mores, and political and criminal enemies. Today we have a Bond who weeps and bleeds, who does not smoke and does not care whether his cocktail is shaken or stirred; Connery, let alone Fleming, would never have seen him that way.

In addition to the actors there have been a small army of producers, directors and co-stars helping to mould the changing roles of Bond, his allies and enemies. Cubby Broccoli was central among these, setting out to 'fix' what he perceived as the filmic flaws in the books. The inspired, semi-futuristic set designs by Ken Adams placed Bond in an extraordinary new world. Another key influence was Terence Young, the director of the first two Bond films, whose part in shaping the screen Bond is seldom fully acknowledged. Young had served as an army intelligence officer, and both before and after the war the film-maker cut a swathe through Soho in a succession of fast cars and expensive suits, with a parade of beautiful women on his arm. Young to some extent modelled his suave lifestyle on that of Eddie Chapman – aka wartime double agent 'Zigzag' – a professional criminal who had been a close friend before the war. When he was picked to direct *Dr No*, Young is said to have used himself as a model for the part. The late Lois Maxwell (the first Miss Moneypenny) observed that 'Terence took Sean under his wing. He took him to dinner, showed him how to walk, how to talk, even how to eat.' Connery biographer Robert Cotton writes that 'some cast members remarked that Connery was simply doing a Terence Young impression.' Here is yet one more testament to the strange blending of fact and fiction: the definitive film Bond is based on a director who modelled his own lifestyle on that of a spy who was almost certainly known to Ian Fleming in his wartime role in naval intelligence. With pleasing circularity, the film adaptation of Bond may even have impinged on the books Fleming wrote after Connery had taken on the role: in *You Only Live Twice*, published in 1964, Bond seems to have developed a sense of humour, and some Scottish ancestry to go with his new-found accent. Even for his creator, Bond is a changeable, malleable quality.

With great good sense, Fleming observed the film transformation of Bond from a wry distance, though he found the whole process an intriguing 'riot'. In March 1961, he decided to observe it at first hand, arriving on the set of *Dr No* in Jamaica just as Terence Young was filming the moment when Ursula Andress erupts from the sea in her bikini.

Accompanied by Ann, Stephen Spender and the writer Peter Quennell, Fleming blithely walked up just as the cameras were about to roll. Young shouted at them to lie down, and all four obediently hurled themselves into the hot sand. Half an hour later, the creator of Bond and his distinguished literary friends were still lying there, immobile, because no one had told them to get up. I can no longer watch the Ursula Andress bikini scene without also hearing Fleming, giggling in the sand, just out of camera shot.

Fleming attended the premiere of *Dr No* in London on 5 October 1962 (he had already seen the film at a private screening). With the Cuban Missile Crisis hotting up, the threat of nuclear Armageddon struck an immediate chord, and the film was a success, if not yet a smash. A year later, Fleming was present at the premiere of the second Bond movie, *From Russia with Love*, a box-office triumph. On watching the film, John Betjeman wrote to the author, congratulating him on creating a fictional world as complete and absorbing as that of Sherlock Holmes: 'This is real art.' Fleming was unfailingly complimentary about the films, as well he might be, for their success had a galvanising effect on his book sales. Bond expert Henry Chancellor has calculated that in 1960 Fleming was selling an impressive 6,000 paperbacks a week; four years later, with the two films and John F. Kennedy's endorsement of *From Russia with Love* as one of his favourite books, sales had leapt to 112,000 a week, and Fleming was enjoying a tenfold increase in his income. By the end of 1963, in the UK and the US alone, some seventeen million Bond paperbacks had been sold.

Fleming once remarked that he wrote 'chiefly for pleasure, then for money'. The money began to pour in, just as the pleasure was waning. As his body began to fail, crunching out the words, once so easy, became increasingly taxing, a painful chore. To Plomer, he confided that he was 'terribly stuck with James Bond . . . I used to believe – sufficiently – in Bonds & Blondes & Bombs. Now the keys creak as I type & I fear the zest may have gone . . . I shall definitely kill off Bond with my next book.'

He never did, of course. Bond is immortal, but Fleming was not. Typically, he both mocked and trumpeted his own phenomenal success. 'My contribution to the export drive is simply staggering,' he said. 'They ought to give me some sort of medal.' Yet, as he admitted, and his friends knew, he was 'running out of puff'. With one last, courageous effort, in January 1964 he tapped out the first draft of *The Man with the Golden Gun*. Where once he stormed through two thousand words a morning, he was now writing painfully, for a little over an hour a day, and then staggering to an exhausted halt.

Soon after returning to England, he played a round of golf at Huntercombe in Oxfordshire despite a heavy cold (and Ann's remonstrances). The cold turned into pleurisy and he was admitted to hospital, to be diagnosed with a severe blockage of the pulmonary artery. He did not go gently, telling Ann that he 'must get back to life or else'. For a few months more he held on, and then on 12 August, the day of his son Caspar's twelfth birthday, at the age of fifty-six, he suffered another massive heart attack and died.

'I shall use my time,' Fleming had declared, refusing to alter his lifestyle simply to extend his days. Few writers have used a little time more productively. The year after his death saw the sale of no less than twenty-seven million copies of his books in multifarious languages. James Bond had already inspired, and continues to inspire, cartoon strips, imitators and parodists, from Cyril Connolly to Austin Powers. Fleming thoroughly enjoyed the satire, knowing that both imitation and mockery are sincere forms of flattery. He even wrote his own self-parody, another best-seller, for what is *Chitty Chitty Bang Bang* but a story about a man with the rank of commander and a gadget-filled car, on a mission against an evil foreign power. In the film, Commander Pott falls for a woman called Truly Scrumptious, a delightful echo of the Bond Girls' names, and his advice to his children was pure James Bond and, for that matter, Ian Fleming: 'Never say "no" to adventures. Always say "yes", otherwise you'll lead a very dull life.'

In another oblique compliment, critics on the opposite side of the Iron Curtain condemned Bond as an imperialist lackey, and Fleming for creating a 'nightmarish world where laws are written at the point of a gun'. A Bulgarian writer, Andrei Gulyashki, came up with a communist version of

James Bond named Avakum Zakhov. Here was fiction overtaking fact, the Cold War being fought out in rival novels. The language of Bond has entered everyday parlance: his catchphrases, and those grafted on to him by the films, are among the most recognisable in the world. It is almost impossible to drink a vodka martini without remembering Bond's recipe. James Bond could, and did, sell virtually anything: from tea towels to toiletries, cufflinks to chewing gum. But above all he sold an ideal sort of Englishman, the chiselled, deathless, impossibly attractive British secret agent, with a licence to kill, and to love. If the films extended Bond's world in one medium, then the continuation novels authorised by the family gave him endless life in another. The first official imitator was Kingsley Amis, with *Colonel Sun*, in 1968; between 1981 and 1996 John Gardner wrote fourteen James Bond novels; he was followed by the American writer Raymond Benson, while Charlie Higson successfully took on the challenge of writing the Young Bond series, and Samantha Weinberg took the myth in another direction with *The Moneypenny Diaries*. The novelist Sebastian Faulks has now joined the party, with the latest authorised Bond novel, *Devil May Care*, published to mark the centenary of Fleming's birth.

One might expect Ian Fleming himself to have become lost in the huge branding and marketing industry that is James Bond, but he is still there, in the firm jaw of his hero, the punchy prose, the style, the love of things and the sheer craftsmanship of the original writing. He is there, too, in the peculiar mixture of reality and fantasy that is the essence of the Bond books, and the reason for their enduring appeal. Few novelists have given so much pleasure, for so long. Mention the name James Bond to almost anyone, anywhere, and they will smile. Many writers now do what Fleming first did, but nobody does it better. One hundred years after Ian Fleming's birth, James Bond is fifty-six, the precise age that Fleming was when he died, much too young. But 007 is still young, and ageless.

009

THE SPY WHO NEVER DIES

The Spy Who Never Dies

According to *The Times*, scientists are predicting that fifty years from now we will all be living on anti-ageing drugs and communicating with fish. This is, of course, speculation, so let me offer a safer prediction: half a century from now we will all still be watching James Bond films. And so will the fish. As long as they are British fish. And male.

Bond was born with an anti-ageing drug in his fictional veins that is unique in our culture. Sons, as they grow up, progressively decline to do things with their fathers: they grow out of the bedtime story, they would rather go to the football match with their mates. But rare is the son, aged eight or eighty, who will not agree to accompany his father into the fantasy world of 007.

The power of the shared Bond ritual offers a peculiar insight into the masculine British mind. Many women also enjoy the movies, and the appeal of Bond is global, but in order to be both shaken and stirred by Bond (OK, that's the last of the catch-phrases) it helps to be British, male and slightly naff: interested in gizmos, sex without commitment, saving the world, clunking *double-entendres*, fast cars, drink, ironic self-mockery and, above all, embracing a particular sort of loneliness.

It matters not who Bond is, nor which generation he addresses. He may be blond or brunette, bloodless or bleeding. It makes no difference. Every Bond is outside society's rules while saving society itself; he is a stud-muffin, but essentially alone; he has signatures – cars, clothes, watches – but few personality traits or quirks (compare him, say, to the sheer oddness of Sherlock Holmes, or the flaws of Philip Marlowe). He has no politics, no friends, no family, no past (though the new movie tries to build one retrospectively) and no future. He is what many Englishmen imagine they could be, and very seldom are: the lone wolf.

This central core of male fantasy transcends the various incarnations of Bond. He is about having what you are denied in a British world of convention and order. When *Casino Royale* was published in 1953, food was still rationed in Britain and gambling illegal outside exclusive clubs: so Bond played the baccarat tables and ate beef in Bernaise sauce, now the staple of every Angus Steak House, then the stuff of gastronomic dreams. Sean Connery's cold-eyed killer and misogynist transported a generation of british boys brought up on Airfix models, marmite toast and monogamy.

Roger Moore, the most ironic Bond, took cinema-goers from grey Britain to places where the sun shone permanently and you could ski backwards firing a machinegun. Bond has a fabulous wardrobe without ever once having to go shopping – another fantasy for the average British male.

It is fashionable to declare that each generation gets the Bond it deserves. More striking, it seems to me, is just how similar the Bonds have been, which helps to explain the trans-generational appeal. The technology, girls and scenery change. Bond has survived the Cold War, the Vietnam War, two Iraq Wars and several sexual revolutions. Ian Fleming's humourless Bond ('sex, snobbery and sadism', said Paul Johnson, back in 1958) gives way to the politically corrected Daniel Craig version, yet the character is essentially the same.

This is because Bond is a post-war British fantasy, a psychological salve for an imperial power in slow decline – again, something that preoccupies British men, in my experience, far more than women.

Bond is not a spy, in any realistic way, but a political fixer, the embodiment of the hope that Britain still plays a vital part out there, although unseen, in what is essentially an Anglo-American alliance against the evil villains. Osama bin Laden is far closer a Bond villain than more conventional state enemies: the lone billionaire with a megalomaniac plan. It is surely no coincidence that military targets in Iraq have been codenamed Goldfinger, Blofeld and Connery.

In *Casino Royale*, Bond 'reflected that good Americans were fine people and that most of them seemed to come from Texas'. Tony Blair could not have put it better. (Note: James Bond also went to Fettes public school, the Prime Minister's alma mater, having been thrown out of Eton after some 'trouble with one of the boys' maids'.)

The academics have long sought to capture Bond. To the Nietzscheans he is the übermensch personified: 'the devotion of the greatest is to encounter risk and danger and play dice with death'. To others he is simply a marketing tool, 'the gentleman consumer'.

I think the appeal is simpler: so far from being the ultimate British man, Bond is the opposite of most British men. Where most of us are tongue-tied, sexually timid, ill-dressed, unfit, gentle, defined by friendships and family, and generally anxious, he is violent, smooth, empty and supremely fatalistic. Nothing that happens surprises him; British men are, on the whole, allergic to surprises.

British males love him not because we really want to be like him, but because we know we never will be: the Bond model fulfils a sense of irony that is far more British, and fits us much better, than any Savile Row suit. British men and their sons will enjoy Bond together, forever, because he is not really British at all.

Lest this sound like one of those laments for masculinity, consider this: Ian Fleming wrote *Casino Royale* because he wanted to emulate his successful brother, the writer Peter

Fleming, and to impress his wife's smart literary friends, like
Evelyn Waugh. Needless to say, he didn't.

The irony is that by aspiring to literary respectability –
by imagining he wanted to be something that he evidently
was not – and failing, he achieved something far more lasting:
the ultimate un-Brit, a cultural immortal, and between male
generations a lasting bond, James Bond. (Whoops, sorry.)

010

THE THRILLER WRITER
WITH THE GOLDEN TOUCH

The thriller writer with
the golden touch

A faint whiff of literary snobbery accompanied the news that
Sebastian Faulks has written a new James Bond novel. 'No
one tipped the acclaimed serious literary novelist . . . to be
entrusted with the latest incarnation of Britain's most famous
spy,' one newspaper noted. Another sniffed that replicating
Ian Fleming required an ability to write 'bouts of genteel
sex at bestseller level'.

Martin Amis, on Radio 4, noted that his father, Kingsley
Amis, completed the first 'continuation Bond' in 1965. 'After
he divorced my mother, Kingsley was so churned up
emotionally that he couldn't write anything more serious
than James Bond,' Amis said.

The subtext of all this was clear: the James Bond novels
are not serious literature. Writers of a higher brow have
always wrestled with Bond, trying, and failing, to consign
him to pulp fiction. Yet nearly a century after Fleming's

birth, and more than half a century after he sat down to write, Bond remains a literary landmark of the modern age. So far from being mere adventure stories, the Bond books created an entire fictional world around a single individual, as enduring and rich as those of Sherlock Holmes or Bertie Wooster.

That a literary novelist of Faulks's calibre should take on Fleming's mantle is a fitting tribute to one of Britain's greatest thriller writers. That assessment of Ian Fleming has been, is and probably always will be hotly disputed. Many readers have been neither shaken nor stirred by James Bond in book form, but enraged and offended: by his perceived misogyny, materialism, violence and sexual coldness.

Ever since the publication of *Casino Royale* in 1953, debate has raged over whether Fleming's novels are titillating pop culture with a cruel edge, or a higher art.

During his lifetime, Fleming's detractors included the likes of Cyril Connolly, Evelyn Waugh and Malcolm Muggeridge. The latter hammered Bond as 'utterly despicable; obsequious to his superiors, pretentious in his tastes, callous and brutal in his ways'. Paul Johnson, in a devastating *New Statesman* essay of 1958 entitled 'Sex, Snobbery and Sadism', described *Dr No* as the nastiest book he had ever read. Fleming himself did not help matters by his diffident attitude towards his own creation: this 'thriller thing', his 'oafish opus', the 'pillow book fantasies of an adolescent mind'.

Bond is a medical as well as a literary miracle. In our

health conscious times, 007's louche lifestyle seems more of a threat to his health than any number of SMERSH assassins. At the start of *Casino Royale*, Bond is tucking into his 70th cigarette of the day, while sucking down endless bottles of champagne and weapons-grade martinis made from three measures of Gordon's gin, one of vodka and half a measure of Kina Lillet, a wincingly bitter aperitif heavily fortified with quinine. It is amazing Bond could stand up, let alone drive his Bentley.

But Bond has demonstrated an astonishing capacity for literary survival. Some of the author's more perceptive contemporaries predicted as much. Fleming will still be read, observed Noel Coward, 'long after the Quennells and the Connollys have disappeared'. (Peter Quennell was a prominent critic of the 1940s and 1950s; none of his books is in print today.) Bond has seen off every rival. Bulldog Drummond was put down two generations ago; John Buchan creaks with age; Sax Rohmer's Dr Fu Manchu has not survived the passage of time and the evolution of racial attitudes.

But Bond still lives and breathes, without wheezing.

Fleming's vivid descriptions fire off the page; his plots still cruise along at souped-up Bentley speed and he writes with a tensile beauty. Above all, Fleming's imagined universe remains believable, though the purest fantasy. As John Betjeman wrote to Fleming shortly before his death: 'The Bond world is as real and full of fear and mystery as Conan

Doyle's Norwood and Surrey and Baker Street . . . This is real art. I look up to you.'

This world – of an emotionally cauterised upper-class British secret agent – welcomed allcomers. John F. Kennedy was reading a Bond novel the night before he was assassinated; so was Lee Harvey Oswald, his killer. Bond offers escapism, but of a serious sort. To the readers of the 1950s, Bond was a promise of glamour and plenty amid postwar austerity, the thrill of sexual licence in a buttoned-up society. In our own time of uncertainty, Bond is still the man who can do anything and achieve everything, an exemplar of what Anthony Burgess called 'Renaissance gusto' in a frightened age.

Raymond Chandler, the only thriller writer to rival Fleming for sheer staying power, identified the three qualities that make the Bond books 'almost unique' in British writing: a willingness to experiment with conventional English, a flamboyant evocation of place and an 'acute sense of pace'.

Fleming has been repeatedly emulated, parodied and 'continued', but never equalled, let alone bettered. Fleming published fourteen books; some twenty continuation novels have followed. A few are good, but none quite captured Fleming's (and Bond's) authentic, smoky and sardonic voice. The skills for that are not those of the thriller writer or the mimic, but the more profound talents of the literary novelist, which is what makes the appointment of Faulks as the newest Bond author so intriguing, and so promising.

Even at the height of his fame, Fleming was modest about

his literary accomplishments. He would have been flattered that Kingsley Amis should be his first authorised heir, and Faulks his latest, but he might not have been surprised at the homage. 'I am going to write the spy story to end all spy stories', he once declared. Ten years later Fleming achieved that self-appointed mission, and wrote the spy story that has no end.

THE BOND BOOKS

SELECTED FURTHER READING

Amis, Kingsley, *The Bond Dossier* (Jonathan Cape, 1965)

Amory, Mark, *The Letters of Ann Fleming* (Harvill Press, 1985)

Benson, Raymond, *The James Bond Bedside Companion* (Boxtree, 1988)

Black, Jeremy, *The Politics of James Bond* (Greenwood Press, 2001)

Chancellor, Henry, *James Bond, the Man and his World: The Official Companion to Ian Fleming's Creation* (John Murray, 2005)

Chapman, James, *Licence to Thrill: A Cultural History of the James Bond Films* (I. B. Tauris, 1999)

Cork, John, and Bruce Scivally, *Bond: The Legacy* (Boxtree, 2002)

Dalzel-Job, Patrick, *Arctic Snow to Dust of Normandy* (Leo Cooper, 2002)

Elliott, Nicholas, *Never Judge a Man by His Umbrella* (Michael Russell, 1991), *With My Little Eye* (Michael Russell, 1994)

Fleming, Peter, *Brazilian Adventure* (Jonathan Cape, 1933), *The Sixth Column* (Rupert Hart-Davis, 1951)

Lindner, Christoph, *The James Bond Phenomenon: A Critical Reader* (Manchester University Press, 2003)

Lycett, Andrew, *Ian Fleming* (Weidenfeld & Nicolson, 1995)

Maclean, Fitzroy, *Eastern Approaches* (Jonathan Cape, 1949)

Minshall, Merlin, *Guilt-Edged* (Bachman and Turner, 1975)

Pearson, John, *The Life of Ian Fleming* (Jonathan Cape, 1966)

James Bond: *The Authorised Biography* (Century, 2007)

Pfeiffer, Lee, and Dave Worrall, *The Essential James Bond: The Revised Authorised Guide to the World of 007* (Boxtree, 2003)

Popov, Duško, *Spy/Counterspy* (Weidenfeld & Nicolson, 1974)

Stafford, David, *Camp X* (Viking, 1987)

West, Nigel, *The Faber Book of Espionage* (Faber, 1993)

Willman, Skip, et al., *Ian Fleming and James Bond: The Cultural Politics of 007* (Indiana University Press, 2005)

Winder, Simon, *My Name's Bond* (Allen Lane, 2000)

INDEX

ACKNOWLEDGEMENTS

This book represents a collaboration between many people and several different groups and organisations, all of whom gave generously of their time and expertise, usually at very short notice.

Kate Grimond, representing the Fleming family, Zoë Watkins of Ian Fleming Publications (IFP), and Terry Charman, historian of the Imperial War Museum, were all kind enough to read the manuscript, saving me from a number of embarrassing errors and omissions. It has been a pleasure to work with James Taylor, Elizabeth Bowers, Ann Carter and the rest of the enthusiastic and expert staff of the Imperial War Museum in assembling the objects and words that most accurately represent Ian Fleming and James Bond. I am also grateful to Meg Simmonds of EON Productions for her help, and to Keith Snelgrove, senior vice-president of global business strategy for EON Productions, for granting permission to reproduce stills from the Bond films and photographs of items from the James Bond archive. Thanks also to Johnny Ring for his elegant photography. *The Times*, media partner of the Imperial War Museum exhibition, generously provided full access to its photographic library and archive; my thanks to Bob Kirwin and Donna Richmond for all their help and advice on pictures, and to News International for permission to reproduce a selection of these. My friends and colleagues at *The Times* have been typically helpful, and I am particularly grateful to the editor, Robert Thomson, and executive editor, Keith Blackmore, for their support of both the exhibition and this book.

Emily Sweet of Bloomsbury and Peter Dawson of Grade Design performed miracles in an astonishingly short space of time to bring this project to fruition. Kate Johnson's copy-editing was, as usual, superbly efficient. Ed Victor and his team of highly trained agents have completed another mission brilliantly. Michael Fishwick, Trâm-Anh Doan and the rest of the staff at Bloomsbury have been, as ever, a delight to work with. Finally, my love and thanks to my family for allowing Ian Fleming and James Bond to move in with us.

Ben Macintyre

A NOTE ON THE TYPE

The text of this book is set in Bembo. This type was first used in 1495 by the Venetian printer Aldus Manutius for Cardinal Bembo's De Aetna, and was cut for Manutius by Francesco Griffo. It was one of the types used by Claude Garamond (1480–1561) as a model for his Romain de L'Universite", and so it was the forerunner of what became standard European type for the following two centuries. Its modern form follows the original types and was designed for Monotype in 1929.

BLOOMSBURY

Also available by Ben Macintyre

Agent Zigzag

One December night in 1942, a Nazi parachutist landed in a Cambridgeshire field. His mission: to sabotage the British war effort. His name was Eddie Chapman, but he would shortly become MI5's Agent Zigzag. Dashing and louche, courageous and unpredictable, the traitor was a patriot inside, and the villain a hero. The problem for Chapman, his many lovers and his spymasters was knowing who he was. Ben Macintyre weaves together diaries, letters, photographs, memories and top-secret MI5 files to create the exhilarating account of Britain's most sensational double agent.

'This is the most amazing book, full of fascinating and hair-raising true life adventures . . . it would be impossible to recommend it too highly'
Mail on Sunday

'Superb. Meticulously researched, splendidly told, immensely entertaining and often very moving'
John le Carré

'It is unlikely that a more engaging study of espionage and deception will be published this year'
The Times

ISBN: 978 0 7475 9283 9 / Paperback / £7.99

Order your copy:

By phone: 01256 302 699
By email: direct@macmillan.co.uk
Delivery is usually 3–5 working days.
Free postage and packaging for orders over £15.
Online: www.bloomsbury.com/bookshop
Prices and availability subject to change without notice.

www.bloomsbury.com/benmacintyre